Today, at one and the same time, scholarly publishing is drawn in two directions. On the one hand, this is a time of the most exciting theoretical, political and artistic projects that respond to and seek to move beyond global administered society. On the other hand, the publishing industries are vying for total control of the ever-lucrative arena of scholarly publication, creating a situation in which the means of distribution of books grounded in research and in radical interrogation of the present are increasingly restricted. In this context, MayFlyBooks has been established as an independent publishing house, publishing political, theoretical and aesthetic works on the question of organization. MayFlyBooks publications are published under Creative Commons license free online and in paperback. MayFlyBooks is a not-for-profit operation that publishes books that matter, not because they reinforce or reassure any existing market.

1. Herbert Marcuse, *Negations: Essays in Critical Theory*
2. Dag G. Aasland, *Ethics and Economy: After Levinas*

ETHICS AND ECONOMY

Ethics and Economy:
After Levinas

Dag G. Aasland

www.mayflybooks.org

First published in 2005 as *Økonomiens grenser og etikkens nødvendighet: En vei til Emmanuel Levinas* by Cappelen Akademisk Forlag, Oslo, Norway.

This translation first published by MayFlyBooks in paperback in London and free online at www.mayflybooks.org in 2009.

ISBN (Print) 978-1-906948-00-9
ISBN (PDF) 978-1-906948-01-6

Contents

Introduction   1

ECONOMIC RATIONALITY
1   The Development of Economic Thought   9
2   Business Ethics   17

SUBJECTIVITY
3   The Subjectivity of Understanding   29
4   The Subjectivity of Literature   41

ETHICS
5   Ethics of Care   55
6   Ethics in the Economy   63

Summary, Conclusion and Consequences   79

Acknowledgements

This book is to a great extent a translation of a Norwegian book published in 2005 (Aasland, 2005). Some changes were made, however, partly due to the transition from a Norwegian to an international context, partly due to some afterthoughts that have occurred to me during the two last years.

The elaboration of the book into an English version came about due to an initiative made by Campbell Jones and MayFlyBooks. I wish to thank both for the initiative and the encouragement. I am also greatly indebted to Armin Beverungen for correcting my insufficient English. I also wish to thank David Bevan for his help with the English language of the first chapter at an earlier stage.

During my work with the Norwegian book I received great help and encouragement from Asbjørn Aarnes, Roger Burggraeve, Ole Andreas Bjerkeset and Aslaug Kristiansen, and from Cappelen Academic Publishers through their editor, Hilde Kristoffersen, whom I all want to thank also on this occasion. Finally I will thank my wife, Helga Aasland, for her continuous inspiration and encouragement.

Grimstad, Norway, July 2007

Introduction

'Ethical failures' in business: why not?

From time to time we are presented with cases in the news media where named business leaders are accused of having done something they should not have done. They may have received gifts or money from business partners or they may have paid to gain an advantage over their competitors. The allegation hidden behind such cases is that a boundary has been crossed; a boundary that is drawn by the laws that are set up to regulate market competition, by some internal guidelines the company has set up to take care of the external image of the company, or by some diffuse ethical rules for what society may allow its citizens.

Confronted with a series of such examples, how should we approach the topic of ethics in business? First, it is hard to tell how singular such cases in fact may be. It is easy to believe that they occur more frequently than what the news media either discover or choose to report. Secondly, in many cases it is actually quite easy to understand why the leaders who are criticised may have acted as they have done. With constant pressure from their owners to achieve continuously better results and with a perspective where the world, quite naturally, is viewed from their own position and from that of their company, it is often easy to understand why the leader in question may have stretched the boundaries to obtain a highest possible gain, either for themselves or for their company – which, in many cases, is not the same: some 'ethical failures' are made to obtain a personal gain, others are made to obtain a higher gain for the company. Both kinds are often easily understandable, so the reactions which the media seek to provoke in the public may thus easily take the form of hypocrisy. Also, to better

1

understand these cases and how they are presented, it might be useful to see how they play on important aspects of social psychology. Negative reactions from the press and society may be seen to express a deeper, underlying wish among all of us to preserve the idea that such events indeed are exceptions, and that leaders and other decision makers mainly operate within all visible and invisible borders. This idea is important to stick to, as, if not, order should turn into chaos. When we then, once in a while, are reminded that reality is not ordered as well as we want it to be, this is experienced as scary, and in such cases it is a well known human trait to designate scapegoats.

The original scapegoats were real goats designated to symbolise the sins and the bad consciences of the people, and then chased out in the desert to die (Leviticus 16: 8-10). Later, through history, many kinds of scapegoats have been appointed who have threatened the ruling order, with witch burning as one of the worst examples. The question of who are the 'witches' of today, and how they are 'burned' will not be further elaborated here; I shall leave that to the readers to reflect upon. Concerning business leaders, however, we note that the normal procedure is to remove him from his position (for simplicity of expression I choose to refer to the business leader as 'he'), paying him a considerable amount, maybe as an excuse that this time it happened to be him who was appointed to play the ritual role as scapegoat. And then, as soon as the scapegoat is out of the way, it is a part of the idea that the problem is gone with him and everyone can go back to the initial order. In this way we may preserve the idea that such disturbances in the necessary order are only singular exceptions.

Let me here, so as not to cause any misunderstanding, make it clear that I do not argue, and even less mean to prove, that such actions are more common than I may have reason to believe; nor shall I claim that the theory of scapegoats is adequate to every case. In this context, it is sufficient to note these moments as possibilities. These possibilities, both that such acts are more common than we usually believe them to be, and that the reactions from society could be rationalised by our need to appoint scapegoats in order to preserve the idea of a good, universal order, makes it possible to obtain a more manageable perspective on the problems concerning ethics, and the lack of ethics, in business and economy. I shall describe this perspective as follows: acts that are criticised as morally bad are actually easy to understand as they in most cases follow directly either from what is considered as being expected from a business leader in the direction of pursuing the financial interests of the company, or from the universally human property of maximising one's own share in the distribution of goods in society. Is it not instead the cases were business leaders and other decision makers resist the temptation to follow the interest of themselves, or that of their companies, which need to be explained? Within the framework of business logic it is of course also possible to explain cases of good behaviour. The relentless pursuit of more profit is of course limited both by legal and market mechanisms, in the sense that a bad reputation may reduce the economic results of the company (and *vice versa*: a good image may improve it); one sanction which leaders try to avoid is being brought into focus for having done something that may be viewed as being on the 'borderline', even if it is not illegal (and maybe instead keeping oneself on the right side of, and in a safe distance to, this border). I shall look closer at these mechanisms in chapter 3; they are thoroughly discussed in the field of knowledge called 'business ethics' or 'corporate social responsibility' (CSR). However, claims that moral limits are created only by legal and economic institutions may be hard to accept, because they threaten the desired idea of the 'good' in man as something more fundamental than social institutions. However, to renounce the assumption of a basic 'good order' in society is not the same as denying the existence of the good, quite the opposite: to take the good for granted may be an efficient way to ignore it.

The easiest thing to understand is that all individuals are closer to themselves and their own wellbeing than to that of others. So much the more important then becomes the question why everyone does not always act according to this. Looking at everyday life it is easy to find examples where people do not at all, at least not all the time, act in the way that is best for them. To observe this, however, we will mostly have to rely on personal experience, as news items in the media concerning benevolent acts do not have the same market value as their opposite, for the reasons already mentioned: we don't want to believe that they are worthy of being cases in the news, as we instead want them to belong to normality. (One should always remind oneself that what is presented in the news media does not mirror the common view of reality, but rather the exceptions from this view).

Two questions and a perspective

Based on the discussion above the question should be asked why one would be interested in doing something other than that which gives one the highest gains. To be more precise, I shall divide this question in two:

1. From where does the idea that it is possible to do otherwise than privileging oneself over others come?

2.This idea, which we may call 'the idea of the good', or, as we will call it here, *ethics* – how is it transformed into practical conduct?

In this book these two questions will be approached step by step, with the purpose of arriving at possible answers. The approach to ethics in business described above, leading to the two questions, also implies a perspective that is somewhat different from how ethics commonly is discussed. Instead of asking the unfortunate business leaders 'How could you?', I shall instead ask those who do not bring themselves into such embarrassing positions 'What keeps you from doing it?' In other words, instead of taking the risk to end (or start) up with a moralistic attitude, I shall search for the good which is already there, as small as it may be. Instead of introducing a normative approach through telling others what is right and wrong, I shall instead introduce the normative by considering how the subject – the I – becomes responsible. In this I shall to a large extent lean on the works of the French-Jewish philosopher Emmanuel Levinas. This explains the subtitle of the book: After Levinas. At first sight it may seem contradictory that a book which starts with the history of economic thought and leads up to a presentation of Levinas is titled 'After Levinas'. The explanation is that the whole book is written in the light of the philosophy of Levinas, a light that also casts its beams back onto history and helps us to see it in a new way. One could thus wish that the English word 'after' also had the meaning of 'according to' in the same way as the corresponding French word *après*.

The book is organised in three parts. On my way towards answers to two questions raised above, I shall first consider the logic, the thought and reasoning of business and the economic system. This is the purpose of the first two chapters. I will show how and why economic logic and reasoning is based on self-interest. However, this fact itself does not suffice for moral criticism. Rather, it implies that the economic system and its way of reasoning have a limited validity. After having discussed economic thought in general, I shall proceed to so-called 'business ethics', a knowledge from which business leaders can learn how they can meet ethical challenges from the environment, and preferably pre-empt them, to the advantage of themselves and their own companies. I will show how this knowledge fits well within the self-centred perspective of economic reasoning and business logic.

The easily recognisable self-centred perspective of 'business ethics' makes it easy for everyone to criticise this field from a perspective of 'real ethics'. However, the two questions posed in the introduction may help us to avoid falling into the 'moralising trap' of an ethical perspective. By what right do I ask another person why he or she fails ethically? As already explained, we will instead ask why ethical failures don't occur all the time. The first part will therefore end with a restating of the two questions, leading us to the question whether it is at all possible to understand ethics, knowing that all understanding is subjective and thus self-centred; in other words, establishing a perspective opposite to that of ethics. Thus, I will explore the phenomenon of subjectivity further, before I return to the two questions once more.

Subjectivity is the theme of the second part of the book, containing two chapters that more or less can be considered as the pivotal point of the line of argument. First, in chapter 3, developments in the theory of knowledge and understanding will be presented, showing how we have learned to cope with the experience that each subject understands reality in his or her own way. Then, in chapter 4, I will show how imaginative literature, here represented by two plays of Henrik Ibsen, may express the subjectivity of ethics in ways that cannot be done in languages constrained by the academic rules of logic and consistency.

From the discussion so far we may perceive that self-interest in general and in economic activities and reasoning especially is indispensable, but at the same time that their validity is limited, as there is no room for the idea that it is possible to do otherwise than pursuing one's self-interest, an idea which I have here named 'ethics'. The third part is dedicated to an investigation into this idea. In chapter 5 I present how ethics (in the sense of the word described above) forms a base for a whole group of professions, formulated as an ethics of either care, relations or closeness, and which is applied in professions of the welfare state in particular. But I will also show how this ethics meets a severe problem in its confrontation with economic reality, which is not only a special way of thinking (in which case the problem would be easier to overcome) but more than that. Then, in chapter 6, I will show how Emmanuel Levinas, through his work, exactly points at how ethics, in the meaning of the idea of the good, in spite of the contradiction between ethics and economic reality, is transformed daily into practical conduct. I then summarise the line of reasoning in the book, followed by a conclusion. I go back to the two questions raised above and suggest answers to them. Finally, I will discuss the consequences these conclusions may have on practical life, politics and the further development of knowledge.

ECONOMIC RATIONALITY

1

The Development of Economic Thought

The historical roots

In order to better understand the logic and way of thinking and reasoning in business and the economic system, I shall begin with a short review of how economic thought has emerged and developed. I shall go back nearly three hundred years in history, to the era known as 'The Age of Enlightenment' in Europe, which more or less coincides with the eighteenth century. In our conventional way of organising our history, that is, the history of Europe, the time of enlightenment succeeded the *Renaissance*; the era of many of the great discoveries, represented by, amongst others, the scientists Nicolaus Copernicus (1473-1543), Galileo Galilei (1564-1642), Johannes Kepler (1571-1630) and Isaac Newton (1642-1727). The Age of Enlightenment was later followed by the era we call 'modernity'. The Age of Enlightenment was a time of liberation and disengagement from authorities in several fields. Common people revolted against serfdom and feudalism, while scientists defied the power of the church in the question of what should be valid knowledge and what should be held as truth. Participation in these kinds of revolt entailed a certain risk. During the Renaissance, for instance, Galileo was persecuted by the church for giving his support to the Copernican theory claiming the Earth is not the centre of the Universe. Revolts against kings and emperors were, of course, also an engagement involving high risk and there was considerable bloodshed during these European battles of liberation. Both the American and the French revolution were strong expressions of this revolt. From the French revolution we all know the slogan 'Freedom, equality, fraternity!' In the American Declaration of Independence of 1776 we find the

9

following formulation, which every schoolchild in USA since then has had to learn by heart:

> We hold these truths to be self-evident, that all men are created equal; that they are endowed by their Creator with certain unalienable Rights; that among these, are Life, Liberty, and the pursuit of Happiness. That, to secure these rights, Governments are instituted among Men, deriving their just Powers from the consent of the governed. That, whenever any form of Government becomes destructive of these ends, it is the Right of the People to alter or to abolish it, and to institute new Government, laying its foundation on such Principles, and organizing its Powers in such form, as to them shall seem most likely to effect their Safety and Happiness. (Hancock *et al.*, 1776: 510)

It is easy to read between the lines in such declarations the strong need of revolt but also the great enthusiasm and optimism which accompanied these efforts of liberation.

One of the most epoch-making ideas in that time was that of individual freedom and rights. Already during the Renaissance René Descartes (1596-1650) had worded the sentence '*Cogito, ergo sum*', meaning 'I think, therefore I am'. By this statement, Descartes meant that because I think, I can also know that, if nothing else is so, at least I exist. This insight stimulated not only a further development of the theory of knowledge driven by the thinking subject, but also developments towards a clearer consciousness of the I, as an autonomous being with freedom to think, and not at least to speak, whatever he or she wills.

The technical inventions of that time along with the liberation of the I prepared the ground for what has been called 'The Industrial Revolution', which again stimulated the natural sciences to their great triumphs. In this way there exists a continuous line from the Renaissance through the Age of Enlightenment to modern time, where one could imagine that the individual, with help from the conquests of science and democratic governance, should liberate him or herself from all suppression, where sufferings and poverty should be abolished once and for all, as these conditions were considered consequences of a lack of knowledge and democracy. This idea was clearly expressed in the constitutions set up by several nations by the end of the eighteenth century: The United States in 1787, France in 1791 (and other smaller nations followed, such as Norway in 1814). Essential points in these constitutions were the freedom of the individual from casual exercise of power, in addition to other rights, such as the right to property, freedom of speech, the right to criticise one's leaders, the right to have a private life and to bring one's cause to the court.

In this enthusiasm about individual freedom and rights, *ethics* was also understood as something that is embedded in each, autonomous individual, as this was formulated by Immanuel Kant (1724-1804). His main work is considered to be *Critique of Pure Reason*, while his main contribution to moral philosophy is *Critique of Practical Reason*. These titles, however, do not mean that Kant was critical of reason in any sense, rather the opposite. According to Kant, reason is what makes us human, not only as rational but also as moral individuals. The word 'critique' indicates Kant's method, which was to let sense experiences and critical thought reciprocally correct each other.

Kant is often associated with the term 'ethics of duty', which may easily be misunderstood. He brought the idea of the autonomy of the individual one step further. He warned against all kinds of obedient subjection to duties imposed from above, whether from the church or the state. In all individuals the moral law is embedded as part of their practical reason. Thus, there must be a free will with which the individual, through reason, chooses to follow the duties prescribed by the moral law. The moral law is a universal principle, meaning that it does not distinguish between persons, and Kant formulated it as what he called 'the categorical imperative': *Act only according to that maxim by which you can at the same time will that it would become a universal law.* This is not a principle he claims to have invented; it has always been there; his contribution was to help formulate it. It follows from the categorical imperative that the ethics of Kant values the purpose and intention of an act more than its consequence and result. Kant was optimistic in his view of the future of social development. By nature, humans are neither good nor bad; we are by birth not moral beings, but follow our inborn natural inclinations. But we become moral individuals when reason develops within us through the concepts of the moral law. By developing our moral freedom to follow the moral law we can liberate ourselves from the determination of the world and create a good society with freedom and a government based on the will of the people, as it is for instance expressed in the American Declaration of Independence, which was written exactly at his time.

11

Economic science

Economics as a science developed in the wake of the idea of the liberation of the individual combined with a scientific approach – ideas that had been so successful in natural science and engineering. We can imagine that the following question was asked: when I now have achieved the freedom to choose what I mean is to my own best, how can I then in the best possible way use the resources and technology available to obtain the best possible life? The attempts to answer this question, either in the role of producer or consumer, developed what is called 'object rationality', or also 'means-end thinking'. The characteristic of this kind of rationality and way of thinking is that one starts with identifying goals and means, where the means normally have to be distributed towards several, alternative goals. Through this way of thinking a so-called *instrumental knowledge* developed, which is a knowledge that, after having identified goals and means, searches for how to obtain a maximum of the goals with the given means; or, alternatively, how to use a minimum of means to obtain a given goal. Such 'means-end thinking' is something we perform daily without reflecting much on it, and it is indispensable for managing everyday life.

A textbook illustration that has often been used to demonstrate the paradigmatic issue in such instrumental, economic knowledge is Daniel Defoe's novel *Robinson Crusoe*, about the man who was shipwrecked on a deserted island: given certain amounts of natural resources and his own manpower, how should Robinson spend his time between, respectively, producing means of production, consumption goods and 'take out' leisure time for consumption?

On this background we may very well say that economic knowledge is 'knowledge for utility and pleasure'. This is also supported by the school in philosophical ethics called *utilitarianism*. Utilitarianism is about maximising the welfare of individuals, and thereby also of society as a whole. It is usually associated with the formulation 'a maximum of happiness for a maximum of people'. As an ethical theory, and especially suited as a super-structure for economic science, it has been based on mainly the works of the two British philosophers Jeremy Bentham (1748-1832) and John Stuart Mill (1806-73). As opposed to Kant, who valued the inner, moral law of the individual, and thereby focused on the *purpose* of an act, utilitarianism values the *consequences* of an act, to oneself as well as to others.

Within economic knowledge *efficiency* has become a crucial value. Efficiency may be defined as absence of waste, that is, a situation where it is impossible to use the given resources differently in a way that gives a higher attainment of the particular goals. Which products give the highest satisfaction, and how there should be prioritisation between them – in other words, what is to be maximised – is up to the individual, free consumer to decide. This is done by letting each individual dispose of his or her own money, earned as income from his or her labour or capital, in a way that presumably gives him or her the maximum utility and pleasure. It is the market mechanism that takes care of the aggregation of all these individual choices to the best for all, that is, for society. Adam Smith (1723-1790), the founder of economic science compared this market mechanism with an 'invisible hand', actually discussing the preferences of merchants to direct their resources in support of domestic (rather than foreign) industry.

> Every individual… neither intends to promote the public interest, nor knows how much he is promoting it. By preferring the support of domestic to that of foreign industry, he intends only his own security; and by directing that industry in such a manner as its produce may be of the greatest value, he intends only his own gain, and he is in this, as in many other cases, led by an invisible hand to promote an end which was no part of his intention. Nor is it always the worse for the society that it was no part of it. By pursuing his own interest he frequently promotes that of the society more effectually than when he really intends to promote it. I have never known much good done by those who affected to trade for the public good. (Smith, 1976: 456)

It is easy to imagine how this vision of a perfectly functioning market inspired people with a special interest in mathematics to put the entire market mechanism in a formula. This is also what was done, not long after Adam Smith proposed his theory.

With regard to the common tasks of society, it became a common agreement within economic science that the government at least would have to decide on both the extent and the content of these common tasks. These decisions, however, would of course have to be made by a democratic political system. For the state authorities instrumental knowledge also became a useful tool. Methods were developed which could quantify total social utility and total social costs connected with possible public projects, such as road constructions, in order to rank all

13

alternative projects by the difference between utility and costs. The method for calculating social utility and cost values and how to aggregate them is in economic science known as *cost-benefit analysis*.

From a social to a corporate perspective

On exactly this question concerning the participation of the state in the economy, there have been great changes during the last twenty years. In November 1989 the Berlin Wall fell. This event marked the climax of a long-lasting process of an increasing discontent and resistance among the population in Eastern Europe and the Soviet Union against inefficient and undemocratic state-governed regimes. This historical event had its parallel in the West, with small 'Berlin Walls' falling in a sequence of events. For some time there had in the West accumulated a certain dissatisfaction about, and a weakened trust in, a large state bureaucracy that did not manage to deliver the services which were expected from it, and in an efficient way. The expectations of the state to be a 'super responsible' supplier of welfare goods grew faster than its ability to meet these expectations. In each nation there grew an increasing support for a larger use of the market in society, a view that was expressed as an increased support for the political right (a movement that has been especially connected to the president of the USA from 1981 to 1989, Ronald Reagan, and the prime minister of Great Britain from 1979 to 1990, Margaret Thatcher), leading to so-called 'deregulations' in several sectors, such as the energy sector. In the news media, the content of 'economic knowledge' became more business administration and less economics. Business schools took over much of the role of delivering premises for economic politics which earlier had been that of economics departments in universities. This change in roles also implied a change in the common understanding of economic knowledge. While economics primarily used to provide tools to governments for its various projects of modernisation at the national level, geared towards a quite complex goal of increasing the welfare of the population as a whole, business administration provides tools elaborated for a company in its more manageable efforts to obtain the largest possible gain for itself. The field of knowledge called 'business management' covers in fact much more than accounting and budgeting. It also includes marketing, organization theory, strategic management and other disciplines. A basic property of this change of perspective in the question of what is relevant economic knowledge is that while this knowledge was knowledge for the society; it has now increasingly become knowledge *for* the management of a corporation. What is seen as a relevant part of this knowledge is determined by what knowledge corporate management is expected to possess in order to make the decisions that are best for the corporation; that is, decisions that strike the right balance between expected costs and expected gains for the company, which primarily means the owners. This will be more clearly demonstrated in the next chapter, where we shall deal with the topic called 'business ethics'.

2

Business Ethics

The increased market orientation

In the previous chapter I mentioned how the fall of the Berlin Wall and the collapse of the regimes in Eastern Europe and the Soviet Union led to changes also in the Western world: power was to a considerable extent transferred from nation states to private corporations. This transfer of power has led to an increased *market orientation*, resulting in a greater use of the market and correspondingly less use of government control in the production and allocation of goods and resources. This change is seen at all levels of society:

1. *Locally*, such as when municipalities invite private companies to bid on their social services;

2. *Nationally*, as when the provision of traditionally public goods is 'deregulated', that is, more governed by the market (for instance, as in the energy sector);

3. *Globally*, through the so-called 'globalisation' process.

The increased market orientation has become subject to many political debates and strong criticism and scepticism, as has been expressed by organizations like ATTAC and other initiatives, often generated from a moral engagement on behalf of those who suffer the most from this process. Many people experience the changes as a harder working life, caused by still tougher competition, not only in the private sector, but in the public sector as well.

One reaction from society to this trend has been an increased focus on, and demand for, ethics in business. How should companies treat employees and business partners from other parts of the world from an ethical point of view? A greater focus on ethical values in business from outside has had negative effects on some companies. A bad reputation may have a devastating effect on the market performance of the company. Seen from a business management point of view, this is of course a problem, not primarily ethically, but even more so economically. Business leaders have asked themselves how such situations may be prevented, and they have started collecting and developing knowledge on this question. In this way the field of knowledge called 'business management' has come to include the topic called 'business ethics'. This topic is a good example of how business management is able to absorb trends in society, in this case an increased interest in ethics, and through this absorption make it less threatening to business life itself.

As a consequence of the demand on the business community, most of what is presented as 'business ethics' describes a rational accommodation within the logic and the goals of business management, based on the acknowledgement that if the company is to obtain its goals with respect to economic results, it needs to know its own surroundings and how the various players in the social environment will react to the decisions that are made. Such knowledge is necessary because in their surrounding there are media, organizations, competitors, customers and political groups who may be able to prevent the companies from obtaining their strategic and economic goals and in the worst case ruin their business.

Some main topics in business ethics

As with most other knowledge in the field of business administration, 'business ethics' originated in the USA; however, a European version has developed over time. A more close reading of the literature, both the American and the European, though, leaves the reader with an unanswered question: Is 'business ethics' a knowledge of 'ethics *for* business' or is it a knowledge of 'ethics *in* business'? A recently published book written with the ambition to present the European version of this 'business ethics' (Crane and Matten, 2004) opens by describing ethics as "the application of reason to elucidate specific rules and principles that determine right and wrong for any given situation.

These rules and principles are called ethical theories" (2004: 11). Such a description of ethics may be useful if what is needed is an ethics *for* business, as a part of *instrumental knowledge*, but at the same time it creates a need for knowledge about ethics *in* business, which we could define as incidents found in business being alternative to that of pursuing one's self-interests.

According to Crane and Matten the two main challenges in business ethics are problems related to: (1) *globalisation*, defined as "the progressive eroding of the relevance of territorial bases for social, economic, and political activities, processes, and relations" (2004: 16); and (2) *sustainable development*, which they define as challenges referring to "the long-term maintenance of systems according to environmental, economic and social considerations" (2004: 24). These two challenges become even clearer in the authors' attempts to define a European version of business ethics, different from what is seen to be the US version. The European version of the subject is claimed to be less individually oriented and to a larger extent dealing with other agents than the company itself and its owners, such as local and national authorities (and the European Union), labour movements and other stakeholders. Further, European business ethics is more concerned with social issues and negotiated frameworks, while ethics in the US is more concentrated on misconduct and immorality in single decision situations and also in more formal corporate codes of ethics (2004: 27-29).

The question of what term is to be used to describe this knowledge has become an issue in itself. This is of course an important question, in terms of the description of reality as well as the social duties of a corporation. One reason for the continuously ongoing process of finding new words and terms is that people within business life have never been quite comfortable with terminology that has been created and used by others, outside business, such as academics or politicians. The very use of the term 'business ethics' and the increased attention it has received, may give the impression that this is something new, while business people will claim that this is not new at all, and that there is no reason that this should be focused on now more than before. Being confronted with the word 'ethics' by outside society may, for practitioners in business, be experienced as being 'looked down on'. For this and other reasons new terms have been suggested, and one of those that has become widely accepted both inside and outside business is 'corporate social responsibility' (CSR). During recent years another term has been suggested: 'corporate citizenship'. This label tries to cover the most important part of business ethics, especially its European version. The term indicates that corporations have taken over tasks that were earlier assigned to governments (in accordance with the trend described in the previous chapter about the change from a national to a corporate perspective on the economy). This change is especially valid for the two main challenges mentioned above, globalisation and sustainable development. The term 'corporate citizenship' is also well suited for other properties of the European version of business ethics (see Crane and Matten, 2004: 62-63).

It is also worth mentioning how business ethics (or whatever one chooses to call it) treats the various established ethical theories. Usually one chooses a rather pragmatic approach to these theories. Various ethical schools are often described, such as utilitarianism and Kantianism (which are both described shortly above), more or less as 'cafeteria concepts': the reader, and the business leader, may choose the theory that fits best in each case. This is a part of the instrumental perspective of business management. The main interest of business leaders is to find tools that work, more than seeking the truth about humans and their views on right and wrong, in other words the question which originally occupied the authors of these theoretical contributions. With such an approach one could perhaps say that business ethics, in the sense of 'ethics for business', is 'utilitarian' in the sense of being utility-oriented in its choice amongst ethical theories. On the other hand, however, the question is whether such a choice is an ethical choice at all. In the end it is the interest of the company and not that of others which is in question. Such a self-centred perspective can hardly be viewed as ethical at all. This illustrates exactly the advantage of making the distinction between 'ethics for business' and 'ethics in business'. The first is not an ethics (because it is for oneself) but instead a part of business administrative, instrumental knowledge, while the second (that is, 'ethics *in* business', which we will say more about later) is an ethics. The intriguing question we will discuss later is to what extent the latter can be presented as a knowledge.

Another central issue in this field of knowledge with its many names concerns the roles, properties and importance of the different stakeholders of the company. Here we find a bundle of agents: shareholders, employees, customers, suppliers, civil society and authorities, only to mention those that are closest. From an ethical perspective, and especially from that which I will choose later, when I shall see how ethics, in the sense of the idea of the good, is put into practice, we can say that such discussions of the various stakeholders is a consequence of the problem that in practical life there are always more than one other to relate to. Put another way: at the moment the subject, in this case the corporate manager, acknowledges that there is not only one other to take care of (regardless who that may be), but more than one, i.e. a third, a fourth etc., then one has to start reflecting, analysing and searching for theories about what the differences are between them and how they are to be handled in the best way in accordance with their roles, their properties and their importance to one's own company.

What is a failure in business ethics?

As mentioned in the previous chapter about business management as the new perspective in economic knowledge, it is expected that a business manager, with the tasks and the responsibility he is dedicated to meet, should make the *right* decisions, in the sense of performing the right evaluations of expected gains and costs for the company. The difference that may be caused by including ethical considerations in these evaluations does not change this: it implies only that how the company meets the ethical challenges from society has come in as added entries to the evaluation – both on the negative side, as reduced reputation and trust, and on the positive side, as improved reputation and trust. Regardless of what counts or not, the decisions made by managers always rest on weighing expected positive against negative consequences. Mistakes in such evaluations are not made because those who make them do not know ethics, but because they do not know their surroundings and their reactions sufficiently. From time to time issues appear in the news media where, for instance, top managers give themselves and each other high wage increases or other financial advantages. What appears as wrong in such cases is that these decisions are made in communities that are too closed, not allowing different views on the matter.

There is an abundance of examples of such errors of judgement, in financial scandals, allegations or unveiling of corruption and excessive and demoralising wages or pensions to leaders, which all obviously turn out not to be to the best of the companies involved. It is important to notice, however, that within the perspective of business management knowledge, such cases become scandals not because there is a conflict between economy and ethics. They become scandals because of the negative consequences they have for the company and the leaders involved. This can (as already pointed out) not even be called consequential ethics, as they do not consider the consequences for others in other ways than how these might lead to consequences for the company itself and its leaders. Such self-centred considerations cannot be regarded as any kind of ethics. The most important thing for the company, and for the business community, is that if the decision makers had had a sufficient knowledge of business management, including knowledge in 'ethics for business', which is also a kind of self-centred management, or, rather, if it had been possible to have such knowledge, there would have been no scandals. Within this frame of understanding there is always a right answer, a right strategy, which is both acceptable and suitable for the purpose, and consistent, and by consequence would have been sufficient to avoid any scandals.

The ability of economic knowledge to justify itself

Within the frame of understanding of economic knowledge, 'failures', as I have argued above, are caused by lacking knowledge about reactions from surroundings and not by a lack of knowledge of ethics. Viewed, however, from society outside the business community, such cases seem often to have their cause in the fact that decision makers consider the knowledge on which the decisions are based to be self-sufficient. Economic and management knowledge has a logical structure where everything has a cause and all unwanted consequences by principle can be avoided, if only sufficient knowledge is acquired. If one then does not consult others than those who operate within the same frame of understanding, the risk is high that it may go wrong.

As is clearly discernible from the literature, and as can easily be expected, it is assumed of business ethics – in the sense of ethics *for* business – that it must be possible to understand, explain and justify a 'correct' act. This is expected because economic and business management knowledge is equipped with a logical structure that can be understood as a feedback mechanism, sometimes described as a 'boomerang effect': it will always pay to behave morally, because if one doesn't, it will hit back at oneself and one's company as reduced trust or a negative reputation. Cases of moral – or immoral – behaviour that do not have such a feedback effect are for this reason irrelevant. This is why ethics *for* business is an instrumental knowledge, as opposed to ethics *in* business, which we may also find, but which is something else, to which we will return later.

In economic theory the market is presented as a self-regulating mechanism. Ethical objections against a company may in the future harm the company, through giving it a bad reputation. Due to this feedback effect the management of the company will lay restrictions on themselves, to avoid negative corrections from outside. For instance a pharmaceutical company which is accused of bribing medical doctors with expensive dinners, travels etc., will by itself tone down such offers, because a bad reputation may harm the company. In other words, the instrumental knowledge we have here called ethics for business tries to find out just how far a company can push, before some reactions from outside will hit back at the company.

One may of course ask the question whether such a self-regulating mechanism is sufficient, so that intervention from outside society will be unnecessary. On the other hand, such interventions may also be viewed as a part of a larger self-regulating mechanism: if the condition becomes sufficiently exposed to criticism, political action will be taken bringing the situation back in balance (perhaps also with the help of a scapegoat mechanism). In this way all theory about society may be considered as a logical, balanced and closed system where everything can be explained. But there is still *one* question that cannot be answered by this kind of theory in general, and by the theory of business and economics especially: where does the idea of the wrong being wrong come from? Or, to put it more positively: where does the idea of the good derive from? Why do people react to corruption, greed, accounting fraud and the exploitation of children and poor people? In other words: what is it that initially triggers the mechanisms in society which at the next turn cause companies to ask for more knowledge about ethics for business? The answer must be found in some universal human reactions that are not contained in conventional knowledge. There must be something in humanity which causes our negative reactions to such acts. Whether it comes from inside or outside the individual (or maybe from a combination of the two), in any case it comes from a place outside the logic of any self-regulating systems. This is why one can also speak about 'ethics in business', as a phenomenon taking place between people in organizations, but which does not fit the descriptions of 'object rationality' and instrumental knowledge. It is exactly this side of humanity that I try to trace in this book.

Business 'ethics' and 'real' ethics

We have seen that what is called business ethics, in the sense of ethics *for* business, may be understood as part of the instrumental knowledge of business management. This does not necessarily mean, however, that this knowledge is irrelevant from a 'real' ethical point of view, nor that it merely serves window-dressing purposes. Business ethics (in the above sense) is in fact the only way ethical considerations can be represented within economic and instrumental management knowledge. Taken into account what impact this management knowledge has, and even more so all the activities that are based on such knowledge, it should be obvious that business ethics, even in this limited version of being ethics for business, is of great importance. Ethics for business describes – and prescribes – the way companies respond to ethical challenges in society, and thus constitutes a crucial part of the knowledge called business management. But still, this knowledge is something other than what we will later call *ethics*.

Let me elaborate this point a little more through an analogy. Within the knowledge that business management has to acquire about society, one cannot presume that consumers are rational. Such an assumption could lead to decisions that do not benefit the company. Business managers realise quite early that consumers are led by irrational incidences and influences. In fact, such irrational incidences and influences are something the companies themselves may use to their own advantage, by appealing to it in their advertising. This knowledge about the 'irrationality' of consumers is analogous to the knowledge of business ethics: when a business manager takes ethical considerations into account before a decision is made, it is, as noted before, because such considerations are a part of the necessary knowledge about the society surrounding the company. To the company, ethics belongs to the category of 'unexplainable behaviour of the surroundings'. It is exactly by acknowledging this that business management demands knowledge called 'business ethics' and 'corporate social responsibility'. Such an 'ethics' has become rational knowledge about irrational society 'out there'. In other words, business ethics does not change the condition that forces the business manager to be self-centred, even if he or she, as a human being, may be far more multi-dimensional. Business ethics makes this difference even clearer.

Business ethics is about the necessity for a company to be responsive. That means two things: first, the company must be able to respond to demands from its surroundings in the way that is for the best of the company itself. Secondly, the company must also be able to predict how its surroundings will respond to the acts and words of the company, so that these acts and words will not harm the company, but may rather work to its advantage.

In addition to such responsiveness, however, leaders may have another kind of responsiveness, involving themselves as humans. In the wake of the Enron scandal of accounting fraud in the USA, *Harvard Business Review* asked what actually characterises a good board, that is, a board where such scandals would have been stopped within the walls of the boardroom before they had become scandals. Sonnenfeld (2002) refers to an investigation (not surprising to many outside the business community) concluding that the companies who have shown that they can stop such processes before they become scandals have boards that are not primarily characterised by having much of what is considered business management knowledge (including business ethics), but which rather are characterised by creating a climate of trust and candour, fostering a culture of open dissent, treating no issue as undebatable.

Investigations like this one point beyond business ethics as I have described it here. With such characteristics I am approaching what I have called ethics *in* business, the kind of ethics I am searching for in this book.

The two questions revisited

In my introduction I chose two questions as my selection of perspective for this book:

1. From where does the idea that it is possible to do otherwise than privileging oneself over others come?

2. This idea, which we may call 'the idea of the good', or, as we will call it here, *ethics*, how is it transformed into practical conduct?

In other words, instead of the most common approach to ethical questions, which is to ask why ethical failures occur, we ask why they don't occur more often. That is, instead of taking the side of the good and making the bad into my object of study, I take the opposite stance: starting from common business logic and from the common human tendency to always seek to preserve one's self-interest, I have focused on the daily phenomenon that people in general, and business managers especially, resist the temptation to always maximise gains for themselves or their companies. This perspective also helps to keep us away from what we may call 'the moralistic trap' that can also quite frequently be observed in ethical discussion and literature. The moralistic trap is to place oneself on the side of the good, observing and describing 'the others', those who 'fail', whether it is business leaders or other people 'out there'. It is a moralistic trap because it places oneself on an ethically higher level than the others, and thus it is ethically biased already from the outset.

How easy it is to fall into the moralistic trap, and the question of how it can be avoided can only be understood properly by addressing more thoroughly the matter of *subjectivity*. We all look at the world from our subjective perspective. The consequences of this recognition have been discussed in various ways, and the position of objectivism has been, and still is, gradually replaced by different kinds of subjective perspectives. In ethics however, a tradition of objectivism is still the most common, holding some ideals as universal and objectively true. From a subjective perspective, one will soon realise that from this position one is actually looking down on 'the others', to those who are the object of one's study. By the end of this book I hope to be able to highlight the full consequence of subjectivism also in ethics (without ending in relativism). Before coming to that, however, I shall say something more about subjectivity, especially within the realm of understanding.

SUBJECTIVITY

3

The Subjectivity of Understanding

What does it mean to understand something?

Imagine that you have recently been employed as the financial manager of a hospital. Your background is an MBA (master in business administration), you have earlier worked as financial manager in a private company, but you have no experience in the health sector. The first thing you want to do in your new job is to get an insight into what is particular about the activity of a hospital. You visit all departments and you meet representatives from the great number of professions found in a hospital: doctors, nurses, physiotherapists, bioengineers, psychologists, social workers, educationalists, computer engineers, administrative personnel, drivers, porters, janitors, etc. etc. In order to be able to be a good financial manager in such an organization, you want to *understand* the system you are going to work in. But what does it actually mean to understand something? And even more specifically: what are the consequences of the fact that what you want to understand is something that you, being a part of management, are going to lead, and that you are not going to be led by others? How should you, for instance, approach big and powerful groups of professions, such as the doctors, or big and influential unions, such as that of the nurses?

To understand something in this sense, that is, from a managerial perspective, implies among other things that you will be using language to 'capture' your surroundings in order to relate all that is new to concepts you already know. Learning is to relate what is new and unknown to something that one already knows, and your references will be either your education or your earlier work experience. You will, for instance, find it both practical and illuminating from your perspective to consider patients as a kind of 'users', or maybe even 'customers', while within the organization you will discover a strong resistance from health personnel against such terms. They will probably react negatively to this because in their view such terms ignore the patients as humans. (Economists and business people, who really want to provoke health personnel and at the same time expose the limits of their own knowledge, may call the patients 'cost units'.) You will of course not deny that patients are humans, but in your economic assessments you find it both practical and illuminating to regard them primarily as the users of the services of the hospital, in the same way as customers in any company in the service industry. What you are doing is to attach something that from the outset is 'quite different' from everything you know, to something that you already know so that you can *conceive* it as 'the same as' something you already know. The word 'conceive' comes from the Latin word *concipere* which means 'to take in'. It is a combination of the prefix *com-* and the word *capere*, meaning to take or capture (see *The Oxford Dictionary of Word Histories*). In order to make something a part of your own understanding of the world, you must 'capture' it and make it a part of your already existing understanding. Your *understanding* of reality is *your* understanding of reality; it cannot be someone else's. In the centre of this understanding of reality are you, capturing your surroundings with the help of *concepts*. The purpose of elaborating so much on this here is to make clear that any understanding of reality, and especially an understanding having as its purpose to manage what is to be understood, has to be self-centred. To say that as a financial manager your understanding of the hospital is self-centred may suggest negative associations. But it is neither meant here as something negative, nor as being morally blameworthy. Your understanding *must* be self-centred; that is just what I have tried to explain above. But at the same time this also means that such an understanding, just because it is self-centred, has its limitations. Thoughts and acts that are the opposite of self-centred, which we commonly call ethical, and which are important for health personnel when they insist that one must not forget that patients are also human beings, will fall outside of such a self-centred understanding. To the extent that management knowledge is object-rational, it must be of a kind that is both understandable and suitable for its purpose, and thus it must be *for 'my' sake*, in 'my' world, with 'my' managerial goals – while ethics remains as an idea external to this understanding and knowledge, as unintelligible, because it exists for the sake of *the other*.

A good illustration of this limitation of management knowledge caused by its self-centredness is the discussion that followed when one of the most famous advocates for a liberal market economy, Milton Friedman at the University of Chicago, in 1970 wrote that "the social responsibility of business is to increase its profits" (Friedman, 1970). His argument was that it is as humans that we take care of our fellow humans, while business firms are not humans and their task in society is to produce as efficiently as possible. The role of a business manager is to serve the owners of the firm, who have appointed him or her and who can also fire him or her. Social tasks are for the state and volunteer organizations – and for everyone else as long as they don't do it at work. This argumentation by Friedman launched a lively dispute on corporate social responsibility, and it has been a useful discussion in the sense that it has contributed to clarify concepts and made it easier to 'reveal' false statements about corporative ethics and responsibility. On the basis of what has been said earlier in this book it is easy to understand why business managers think like Friedman. Much of what is said and written about ethics in business easily becomes nothing but window-dressing. This still does not, however, prevent ethics *in* business, that is, acts of setting others before oneself, from occuring. In such cases the behaviour of companies may change, and then the company goes beyond Friedman's description of its social responsibility.

The idea that instrumental knowledge such as knowledge in management is self-centred, in the sense that each one is the centre of one's own universe of knowledge, may to some be an unusual thought. However, this idea is not new: it has in various forms been a part of the theory of knowledge ever since ancient Greece. Still, many seem to be trapped in the idea that one, through knowledge, may obtain direct access to an objective, universal truth, which exists independently of the subject possessing such knowledge. Within the natural sciences, this idea will for most people pose no serious problem; it is only in quantum physics and in the philosophy of the foundations of science that one must be careful in assuming that scientific knowledge exists independently of the subject who observes nature and possesses that knowledge. In human and social sciences, however, it has for a long time been acknowledged that all knowledge depends on the 'eyes that

31

see' and that it is not without problems to elevate one subjective understanding to a level more true than others. In these sciences we observe that one has left the perspective of *objectivism* and instead acknowledged that one will have to deal with one or another kind of *subjectivism*. There are in particular three subjectivistic perspectives that should be mentioned:

1. The sciences of *languages and literature* deal with understanding texts that already exist. But what does it actually mean to understand a text? To answer this question one has in these sciences developed what is called a *hermeneutic method*. This can be viewed as a circle: when first meeting a text everyone has a pre-understanding of it. This pre-understanding is gradually adjusted, by entering the depth of the text, then studying all connections (the context) in which the text has come into being, then returning to the text itself, etc. By this method the understanding of the text is continuously corrected in accordance with what at any time is the existing knowledge, in communication with others. The hermeneutic method is related to the German philosopher Hans-Georg Gadamer (1900-2002).

2. *Psychiatry and psychology* is primarily about understanding individuals in mental crises, with the committed purpose to help them. The different kinds of crises have been given different names, determined by the symptoms and attempts at their explanations, such as anxiety, depression and schizophrenia. There are several schools within these fields, partly competing with, partly supplementing each other. Some are closer to somatic medicine than others, with their instrumental approach and method, based on the dyadic concepts of *diagnosis* and *treatment*. Those who are not, but who still direct their attention to the individual in their attempts to understand mental diseases, realise that these sufferings lie latent in all humans, with the difference that those who get ill don't have the same protective mechanisms that others do. For these people mental diseases may be provoked by their discovering the dark and frightening sides of being a human. For instance, experiencing individual *freedom* may have a frightening and paralysing effect. To others everything in life may appear as indifferent and meaningless, and they thus enter an *existential crisis*. The discourse about what it means to be and live as a human, elaborating further on these questions as something common rather than pathological, is called

existential philosophy. The most prominent contributors to this philosophy is the Danish philosopher and religious thinker Søren Kierkegaard (1813-1855) and the French philosopher and author Jean-Paul Sartre (1905-1980).

3. The *social sciences* try to achieve a common understanding of how society functions. However, one cannot have any hope to find out how society actually *is*; such a truth is not accessible to anyone (more than to others). The only possible option is to try to describe how social reality *appears* to the observing, thinking and describing subject. Language and knowledge will thus have to rest on a hypothesis about intersubjectivity, that is, a hypothesis – which will forever remain such – that we in general have a common understanding of the reality in which we are living and working and which we describe and refer to in exchange with each other. This way of approaching social reality is called *phenomenology*, as it is the phenomena, as they appear, that are described. The most prominent persons in the development of phenomenology are the German philosophers Edmund Husserl (1859-1938) and Martin Heidegger (1889-1976). A third one, who was a student of both of these two, and with whom the reader will be further acquainted later, is the French philosopher Emmanuel Levinas (1906-1995).

There is thus no such thing as a neutral and non-subjective description of society. Or, to be more precise: an attempt to make a neutral and non-subjective description of society would in the best case only be an unstructured and completely unintelligible mess of data, in other words an un-worked projection of reality itself. When we impose a structure on a description, in order to understand it, we also impose a purpose, or some other kind of assessment, on it. We all know very well how we, when watching a movie or reading a book, try to distinguish as early as possible, in order to understand the plot, the 'good guys' from the 'bad guys'. A really good story, however, will challenge these efforts of ours, and by that mirror real life: people are both 'good' and 'bad' and life is not as simple as we often want it to be. All 'ordinary knowledge' is in a certain sense *normative*, whether this is expressed explicitly or hidden implicitly behind a purely descriptive presentation. Even what is called 'descriptive theory' is normative in the sense that it always, but often implicitly, has a purpose, so that one can have any possibility to understand what it is about. In the same way as we want to know who are the 'good guys' and who are the 'bad guys', any explanation of a phenomenon – as theory is – in order to be understandable, is directed towards a desired goal: in medical knowledge there is an implicit or explicit value in saying that it is better to be healthy than sick. In economic knowledge there is, in a similar way, a value appraising economic development rather than economic stagnation. In technological knowledge there is an implicit value towards the innovations that promote human welfare more than those who don't, and also a value saying that a successful project is better than an unsuccessful one.

But then we may ask: if there is no objective, neutral knowledge, what is it then that decides what knowledge is? An answer to this question has been suggested by Thomas Kuhn (1970), an answer that has later been regarded as valid knowledge (in other words, his answer contains his own criteria). Kuhn described how knowledge develops in a social community of researchers, where new discoveries are adopted to existing knowledge as long as that is possible. When this is no longer the case, there is a 'scientific revolution'. But before coming that far, a lot of knowledge is neglected because it does not fit in with the existing, conventional knowledge, or what he called the existing *paradigm*. What version of the truth 'wins' may depend on several conditions, such as which explanation has most political power on its side and which has the strongest power of explanation. (This is, naturally enough, an important point made by many feminist thinkers). Anyway, in one way or another we are talking about various forms of subjective, that is, self-centred, knowledge.

Normative knowledge, such as for instance a managerial, instrumental knowledge, also seems to have another limitation in addition to being self-centred. The freedom, the desire from which this knowledge once originated, seems to have been narrowed down rather than enlarged. What happens when we follow an instrumental knowledge seems to be that we are caught in a closed, self-explanatory logic ending up with one, 'right' solution. Let me elaborate a bit on this phenomenon. Gregory Bateson showed that the theory of evolution in biology also can enlighten the way we think. One of his formulations says that an explanation is "a mapping of a description onto tautology" (Bateson, 2002: 77). With this he meant that a description of something is given a meaning by us and can be explained only when we by help of our reason have imposed a logical structure upon it. A 'tautology' is a logical structure that is self-evident, which means some way or another to say that $A = A$. The logical structure of an explanation is not there initially, that is, from nature's side; it is we humans who 'map' the description onto a tautology, so that we can get the problem 'solved' and by that understand and explain what we have seen.

Embedded in all knowledge is a logical structure which we don't always see, but which always hides the conclusion behind the premises. That does not mean that the world is deterministic, but rather that we in our choice of understanding and explanations make it appear so. Because of this, there is a possibility that any instrumental knowledge, or, if one wishes, any 'school knowledge' may be predictable; it becomes closed and excluding towards what doesn't fit in, that which is different. It develops to become an academic and intellectual language game and thus easily becomes boring to those who don't already participate (as, for instance, new students or people from 'practical life').

Later I will discuss more closely how knowledge can be 'saved' from being reduced into an internal language game. But before saying more about this, I will conclude so far by stating that instrumental knowledge, such as management knowledge, is characterised by the following three properties:

a. it is *normative*, that is, it has a purpose; it is directed (from the subject possessing it and his self-centredness) towards something the subject wants to obtain;

b. it is *conventional*, that is, it is commonly widespread, as a substitute for the 'scientifically proven', objective truth, after objectivism has been replaced by some kind of subjectivism; and

c. it is *explainable*, that is, in order to be able to explain what is described, it must be logically consistent.

The development of what is held as valid knowledge described above, viewed as a counterpart to what we here call 'ethics', may also be described as an expression of the duality of *concepts* and *events*. All knowledge is directed towards saying something about concepts, valid for and containing more than one singular event: from singular events we want to deduce something that is valid for all phenomena belonging to the same concept. By doing so we are forced to make equal singular

35

events that cannot be equal, as they are different events, and this is done by the use of language. The same terms and explanations are applied to different events; it is through this that they obtain their *meaning* and it is through this that we obtain knowledge about what *is*. The problem is that life still consists of singular events where two events are never quite equal. By putting singular events together in concepts, what is unique in each singularity will become invisible; some of the circumstances of the event will disappear as the event is reduced to the same as another event within the same concept. This applies also to the uniqueness of a person. Language will always categorise the other, reducing him or her into an object, being the same as others covered by the same concepts. Thus, already in the idea and the calling of attention to what *is*, there is a violation, if it is about another person. To see the other as unique, different from everything (and everyone) else, will thus fall outside every linguistic category, where everything is always identified as *the same as* something else. To see the other as unique will thus belong outside, or more precisely, will be *prior to*, such categorisations, and thus also prior to any language, and by that also prior to what we by help of language express as what *is*. This became, as I will show later, a decisive insight for Levinas.

Postmodernity

Are the three properties listed above valid for *all* kinds of knowledge? Some would probably not agree to that; however, what we in any case can observe is a tendency towards a situation where knowledge of any kind is forced to justify itself, by fulfilling the three criteria above. First, 'what is the purpose?' is asked by parents, students, politicians and others who pay for education. Secondly, it is required that an understanding of something be conventional, if not it will not 'function appropriately' among other people. Finally, it is expected that all knowledge has a logical structure, if not it will only be a description that cannot be understood. (It could be, of course, so-called 'narrative knowledge', but such knowledge must also have a certain built-in logic to be understood; this logic is only less explicit). This tendency in the development of knowledge is of course closely related to the fact that knowledge is becoming a market commodity more and more in demand, and this fact feeds back into the development of knowledge itself. It is easy to find examples of this: in medicine, knowledge is driven less by the concern of what is best for the patient, and more by economic interests, which are paramount in the pharmaceutical industry as well as in the health sector, which are subject to continuous pressure to gain profits and to cut costs. Even the knowledge called 'ethics' has moved, from being primarily a humanistic discipline about what it means to be a human being, to becoming a required professional and business ethics, expected to be a useful tool for professionals, for industry and for public authorities.

To pursue this topic any further would go beyond the scope of this book. But at least we can observe that what seems to happen with knowledge of any kind today is that it is being confined by still stronger requirements towards fulfilling the three criteria above. (Just one indication of this development is the increasing interest in education in business management and the expectations connected to this knowledge, both from students and employers. These rising expectations towards personnel with education in business management, may in many ways remind us of the rising expectations towards state agencies in the 1970s and 80s both in the East and West, which culminated in the fall of the Berlin Wall, as noted in an earlier chapter).

Within the academic world there is a growing concern for an increasing commercialisation of knowledge. This is part of the market orientation we have earlier noted as an ongoing process in society. Knowledge becomes more subject to market conditions, towards a knowledge for the subject itself, about how, on behalf of oneself or one's company one is going to 'make it' in a society becoming more and more subject to market conditions, not only in the private but in the government sector as well.

So we observe, both in research, that is, in the development of knowledge, and in education, that is, in the dissemination of knowledge, that the quality criteria for knowledge are more and more determined by fluctuating market values. This development may indicate that knowledge – and by that also the concept of knowledge – is unstable, that it is in a state of unrest, maybe in a process of dissolution. One may experience that the fixed, hidden truth and deeper meaning slips. Concepts like *truth* and *meaning* seem to be regarded by an increasing number as both unnecessary and old-fashioned. Instead, it is more and more language that keeps knowledge together. Research and education resembles to an increasing degree a language game in which one is invited to participate, and in which one is forced to participate if one doesn't want to be excluded from social communities. 'The grand narrative' about our society is fragmented into small and singular narratives, isolated from each other. Anything can be explained and defended, if one is sufficiently clever in using words (and in particular if one masters the language game within science consisting of 'method' for its own sake). But through this change, paradoxically enough, knowledge also loses its power of explanation. The purpose of knowledge is to be able to find identities and by that to draw differences, using language and concepts. But when every use of language becomes a game where everything can be explained, differences will disappear. This is what the French philosopher Jean-François Lyotard (1984) has called 'the postmodern condition'. When applying such a critical approach to knowledge production, much of the produced knowledge may easily appear as boring and internal. It engages only those who already themselves participate in the language games.

Preliminary conclusion

Business ethics (in the sense of ethics *for* business) belongs to the field of management knowledge. But at the same time it is also a good illustration of the limits of this knowledge. Ideally there is one right solution which is given by the embedded logic and given premises. Instrumental knowledge alone can thus not come up with new and creative solutions. For such solutions maybe what is needed is knowledge that is *neither* normative, *nor* conventional, *nor* explicable – whether it is at all possible to imagine such knowledge. As an example, we may observe what happens when 'innovation' and 'entrepreneurship' have become independent topics in business management knowledge (as it is realised that in these activities lies an important source of higher profits). These topics represent at first something unknown and different, which one then tries to *conceive*. The problem with this knowledge, however, is that through the conception the unpredictability of these phenomena, which is exactly their most important property, vanishes. What is unknown and different is made into 'the same as' something that is known. In the final stage knowledge about innovation and entrepreneurship is made normative, conventional and explicable. Then one has to start over again, developing new concepts and so on, in an infinite sequence of new words and terms. At the moment something is captured by concepts it 'freezes', and we must start afresh with new concepts in our futile attempts to capture the living and the unpredictable that always changes the existing.

On this basis economic science can be said to have a retrospective base of knowledge (actually this applies to all knowledge; it is just more evident in economics than most other disciplines): 'classical' economics, as it was established by Adam Smith by the end of the 1700s (see chapter 1) and which was further developed into what is today called 'microeconomics', shows how any given situation can be described as an equilibrium, as the only possible one, given certain conditions. 'Modern' economics, as it was established by John M. Keynes (1883-1946), and which has been further developed into what is today called 'macroeconomics', chooses as its point of departure the forms of accounting and the equations that must be in force in any practice of accounting. Both these directions in economic science thus take their point of departure in something that already exists, or something that has already taken place. In this sense we may say that the knowledge to which they belong is retrospective.

We noted earlier that at the historical roots of economic knowledge there was a considerable desire for individual freedom. Today this freedom is again asked for. The question is raised where the freedom that was initially the driving force in the development of economic knowledge has gone. People feel trapped in an economic logic giving them but one 'choice', and thus no real choice at all; a 'choice' consisting of joining the 'merry-go-round' as much as one can both in work life and as consumers, to many people at the cost of their well-being and even health. But if economic knowledge shows us only one 'right' solution, what are the alternatives? On the other hand, there does not appear to be any alternative economic system to choose. Paradoxically enough then, maybe *ethics*, as an idea of being and acting, not for one's own sake but for that of some other, may recreate freedom? Maybe it is because its foundation is more 'true', because ethics comes prior to logical, and thereby deterministic, language?

To Levinas both freedom and the dream of freedom is something that is experienced within the frame of the restraint implied in being responsible for the other. Maybe market liberalism is about to make the same unfortunate experiences as totalitarian regimes made earlier? In both cases it started with a desire for freedom but ended in the opposite, as freedom was gradually institutionalised. Freedom is corrupted by our need to understand and to make everything fit into universal and logical categories. The challenge is *not* to be captured by this need, but instead to keep the unique, not at least the uniqueness in each individual. This will probably require transcending market liberalism, just as it previously required transcending totalitarianism.

4

The Subjectivity of Literature

Peer Gynt: To be oneself enough

Concerning the field of business ethics I have earlier in this book drawn a distinction between, on the one hand, ethics *for* business, which is the dominating perspective since having become an integrated part of the instrumental knowledge of business management, and, on the other hand, ethics *in* business, as the occurrence of the idea that it is possible to set the other before myself, also within and between business organizations. One way of describing the difference is to say that ethics *for* business is a knowledge that business develops and applies *for itself*. As I have already mentiond, the question could be raised whether it is correct to call this ethics, in contrast to ethics *in* business, which, because it is an ethics, can only be applied and developed *for the sake of the other*.

A good elaboration on the difference between that of being for oneself and being for the other, even applied to business activities, is provided by Henrik Ibsen in his play *Peer Gynt* (first published in 1867), in the first scene of the fourth act.

This scene takes place on the south-west coast of Morocco. Peer Gynt, "a handsome, middle-aged gentleman in elegant travelling clothes, gold pince-nez dangling", hosts four admiring men from England, France, Germany and Sweden, respectively. The scene opens by Peer calling for a toast for pleasure: "If man is made for pleasure, why should pleasure fret you?" The four guests praise and flatter Peer, after which Peer confesses that he has achieved wealth and success exclusively because he has only thought of "his' and 'he" and has also avoided marriage. The German guest wonders whether this 'existence-self-

41

projected' hasn't had any costs, to which Peer, sovereignly elevated above the actual course of events, tells how he almost got married to a girl 'of royal family' (who in fact was the daughter of the Mountain King), but that he escaped although it 'cost blood' (but as the reader and audience – but not the four guests – know from earlier in the play, it was a rather miserable affair). On the question from where he has got his cleverness, Peer boasts of his lack of intellectual training. He has not read much, only adopted what one can use, including religion (there can be little doubt that Ibsen here from his position in Central Europe at that time spoke ironically about the Norwegians), to which the Englishman, still admiring, replied "Now, that is practical!"

Peer has also lived in the USA for some years and he tells how he has made his way to become a *self-made man*. He tells that he has earned good money from slave trade crossing the Atlantic and from the export of 'heathen images' to China (which at that time must have been considered a direct sabotage of the Christian mission and thus immoral, maybe even more so than the slave trade). Actually, it occurred to Peer that what he was doing was at the limit of the acceptable, but, on the other hand, it was difficult to wind up such a brilliant business, as

It's very hard, at any rate
in business of such wide deployment,
providing too, so much employment,
quite out of hand to terminate. (Ibsen, 2007: 56)

Peer lightened his consciousness by expanding the export of heathen images by also carrying missionaries and "provide them everything required, like stockings, bibles, rum and rice", so that the "result was neutralised". "But still for gain?" the Englishman asked, to which Peer replied: "I took my slice. It worked". The business concept was ingenious: The more heathen images that were bought by the Chinese, the more to do for the missionaries. On the question from the Englishman of how it went with "Africa, those wares?" implicitly meaning the slaves, Peer answered:

There, too, the triumph of my creed
I saw the trade was rash indeed
for people entering their fifties.
One never knows how short one's shrift is.
On top of that, the thousand snares

set by our philanthropic crew,
not counting piracy, then there's
the risk from wind and weather too. (Ibsen, 2007: 56-57)

He ended up by buying some land in South America, "kept the final load of flesh, which, by the way, was top-grade, fresh". His story further goes:

They throve, filled out to such a measure
it was, to them and me, a pleasure.
Yes sir; without exaggeration
I treated them as father, friend, –
which paid its own fat dividend.
Built schools, too, for the preservation
of standards of morality
throughout the whole community,
and took good care, or I'd soon know it,
its mercury never fell below it.
Besides, I've stopped both kinds of action
and pulled out of the business there; –
I've sold the lot in one transaction,
plantation, fixtures, hide and hair.
The day I left, I had them come,
the kids and grown-ups, for free rum;
the adults all got tight as hell,
the widows got some snuff as well.
That's why I hope that inasmuch
as the saying isn't just hot air:
that "he who does no foul does fair" –
my trespasses are past, as such,
and, more than most, my faith's worth pinning
on virtues cancelling out the sinning. (Ibsen, 2007: 57)

The German guest, clinking glass with Peer, exclaims:

How bracing is a demonstration
of principle in action, quite
set free from theorising's night
unmoved by public condemnation! (*ibid.*)

Peer then betrays his 'business secret', which he by the way shares with his Nordic friends, and which is always to "make sure that you leave a bridge to yield a route by which you can withdraw." Besides, he has

43

always picked some knowledge here and some there, from all the countries he has visited.

Peer is then asked by his guests what he will do with his wealth, since, as the Englishman puts it: "Who'd waste an hour on hoisting sail for sailing purely? Some sort of goal you must have, surely. And that goal is – ?"

To this Peer discloses that his goal is to be emperor over the entire world. Only that can be the realisation of "the Gyntish Self":

> The Gyntish self – It is that host
> of wants, desires that stir one most, –
> the Gyntish self, – it is a sea
> of whims and needs and urgency,
> whatever stirs my breast precisely,
> and thereby makes me live – concisely.
> But as our Lord has need of dust
> to ply his art as world-creator,
> even so for me, gold is a must
> if I'm to look the imperator. (Ibsen, 2007: 59)

In order to obtain this goal, however, more gold is needed. And the latest idea of how to earn more money he got from that day's newspaper. He there learned that the Greeks had revolted against their Turkish rulers, and from this Peer saw good opportunities to gain more wealth. At this point of the party a misunderstanding occurs between Peer and his guests. The guests believe that Peer is now entering the conflict on the side of the Greeks and that he anticipates a reward for this later. They become fully enthusiastic about this idea and they want to join him in the Greeks' struggle for freedom, although with a personal motive of being rewarded, but still fighting for a good cause. They apologise to Peer for having suspected him of being cynical and as they now believe that he will stand on the side of the suppressed Greek people they give him all honour back. To this Peer first reacts with confusion, but then with indignation. Of course will he, Peer Gynt, not choose sides in the conflict. He wants to earn money from the war in the same way he earned money by combining the export of heathen images and missionaries to China: he will supply the Greeks with weapons and at the same time lend money to the Turks, so that the war can last as long as possible. He considers his guests to be quite stupid in not seeing this new ingenious business idea. At this moment he therefore realises that it is time to break up from a pleasant evening, before it turns into the opposite. But before he leaves he explains his position in the following way:

> When one's dominions scarce exceed
> the strip one's body shades, one's rightly
> predestined to be cannon-feed.
> But if one's raised above the mire,
> as I am, then one's stake is higher.
> You go to Hellas. I'll supply you
> arms and transportation, free.
> The more you stoke hostility
> the more I'll gain and profit by you.
> Strike out for freedom and for right!
> You give it to the Turks! Go fight; –
> and end up, to admiring glances,
> impaled on Janissary lances. –
> Excuse *me*, though. *(slaps pocket)*
> I'm worth a mint,
> and I'm myself, Sir Peter Gynt. (Ibsen, 2007: 60-61)

Left alone the four guests become somewhat irresolute. On the one hand, they see great opportunities for profits if they choose to fight on the Greek side and after an expected victory may gain their share in some of the plentiful natural resources of the country. The Englishman tells with great enthusiasm what he has heard about both the copper occurrences in the mountains and the energy of the water falls. But, on the other hand, if they don't emerge victoriously from their engagement:

> but stuck there in the ranks
> we'll drown amongst the mob – no thanks!
> And where's the profit we should save? (Ibsen, 2007: 61)

Finally, the German suggests that they drop this risky project of joining the Greek struggle for freedom and instead choose the far less risky enterprise of robbing Peer's luxury yacht and steal all they may find of valuables there. The others hesitate a bit to get into this swindling, but finally they are led by the temptation of easy money. The whole act ends when also the Swede joins the others with the words:

I have to join their operation, –
but I protest to all creation –! (Ibsen, 2007: 62)

Considering the fact that this play was published in 1867 we may say that the issues in business ethics we have discussed earlier in this book are certainly not new.

A theme throughout the whole play of *Peer Gynt* is that of 'being oneself' as opposed to that of 'being oneself enough'. Peer was told the difference between these two by the old troll of the Dovre mountains ('The Mountain King'), as we can see from the following dialogue in the second act:

DOVRE
What's the distinction between troll and man?

PEER
So far as I know, there is none, by my score.
The big want to roast you, the small ones to scratch you; –
same as with us, if they dare but catch you.

DOVRE
True enough; we're alike in that and more.
But morning's morning, and night is night
so there are differences still, all right. –
Now you must hear what those differences are:
out there, 'neath the shining vault of day,
"Man, be thyself!" is what humans say.
In here with us, between troll-folk, that guff
is expressed as: "Troll, be thyself – enough!"

ELDER *(to Peer)*
Spot the profundity?

PEER
A bit hazy so far. (Ibsen, 2007: 33)

In relation to what has earlier been discussed we could say that 'to be oneself enough' that is, to be like a troll, is to live and to develop and apply knowledge *for oneself*, while that of 'being oneself' is to be a human (and not a troll), where a decisive property of being a human is to encounter another human, that is, to be in an ethical relation. Dedicated to himself and his own life, Peer Gynt had obvious difficulties seeing

46

this difference. One example of this was his reaction when his friends for a moment thought that he intended to join the Greeks in their struggle for liberation, an attitude that many people would consider a consequence of being human.

Later in the play, in the fifth act, Peer asks the figure called 'the button-moulder' what it means to be oneself, and the answer of the button-moulder is: "To be oneself is: onself to slay" (Ibsen, 2007: 112). This answer may appear both enigmatic and rather dramatic (and so is also the figure of the button-moulder). But it can be interpreted such that to be oneself is to set oneself in the background and let the other come forth. For a human to be oneself, as opposed to a troll who is himself enough, it will be to be *for the other*, that is, to renounce oneself. This demand may seem impossible to meet; on the other hand, it is in this being-for-the-other that Peer fails by being himself enough. I will return to these thoughts later, in the presentation and discussion of the philosophy of Levinas.

Another example from the same play is the role of Solveig, who through many years waited for her Peer, and forgave him in spite of all his failures. From Solveig's subjective perspective Peer had been exactly himself, as humans should be, because he had been a person *for her*. To Peer, Solveig was, at the same time, with her patience and unconditioned forgiveness, fundamentally ethical, in the sense of being an '*I-for-the-other*'. They had both been themselves (in contrast to being themselves enough) in the sense of being for the other. In other words, the Peer in the world of Solveig is a different Peer to the Peer who is described in Ibsen's story. Again, we are moving towards Levinas who describes ethics as 'otherwise than being'. Solveig does not judge Peer from a perspective of justice, she shows unlimited mercy, which is prior to any justice. Such interpretation of the end of the play is quite different from what it was the first time it was shown and also as it has been interpreted later: as a banal, hyper-romantic and misogynistic happy end.

The Lady from the Sea: Freedom *under* responsibility

'The Lady from the Sea' is the nickname of Mrs. Ellida Wangel, who, as the daughter of a lighthouse keeper grew up by the open sea. Since then she has always longed for the open sea, a longing that is also connected to her longing for freedom. She is married to a medical doctor who is considerably older than herself, Dr. Wangel, and she lives with him at the inmost end of a long fjord in Norway, far from the open sea. When Dr. Wangel's first wife died and he was left alone with two small daughters, Dr. Wangel asked the young Ellida to marry him, a question which Ellida later reflected upon as if she did not have any choice. Just before this happened Ellida had a romantic affair with a seaman (by Ibsen called 'the stranger'), but he had to escape back to the sea after having committed a murder. Some years later the seaman returns, as he had promised, and asks Ellida to come with him. Ellida feels a strong drive towards the stranger as she also has this drive towards the sea – and towards freedom. She falls into great torment and finally she asks her husband to give her the freedom to choose between him and the stranger. As the situation becomes increasingly tense, Dr. Wangel, who has been both her husband and doctor and considered himself also to be her protector, for the first time sees his wife as an independent human being. The dialogue then proceeds as follows, in the presence of the stranger:

ELLIDA (with growing excitement)
Wangel, let me tell you this – tell it you so that he may hear it. You can indeed keep me here! You have the means and the power to do it. And you intend to do it. But my mind – all my thoughts, all the longings and desires of my soul – these you cannot bind! These will rush and press out into the unknown that I was created for, and that you have kept from me!

WANGEL (in quiet sorrow)
I see it, Ellida. Step by step you are slipping from me. The craving for the boundless, the infinite, the unattainable will drive your soul into the darkness of night at last.

ELLIDA
Yes! I feel it hovering over me like black noiseless wings.

WANGEL
It shall not come to that. No other deliverance is possible for you. I at least can see no other. And so – so I cry off our bargain at once. Now you can choose your own path in perfect – perfect freedom.

ELLIDA (stares at him a while as if stricken dumb)
Is it true – true what you say? Do you mean that – mean it with all your heart?

48

WANGEL
Yes – with all my sorrowing heart – I mean it.

ELLIDA
And can you do it? Can you let it be so?

WANGEL
Yes, I can. Because I love you so dearly.

ELLIDA (in a low, trembling voice)
And have I come so near – so close to you?

WANGEL
The years and the living together have done that.

ELLIDA (clasping her hands together)
And I – who so little understood this!

WANGEL
Your thoughts went elsewhere. And now – now you are completely free of me and mine – and – and mine. Now your own true life may resume its real bent again, for now you can choose in freedom, and on your own responsibility, Ellida.

ELLIDA (clasps her head with her hands, and stares at WANGEL)
In freedom, and on my own responsibility! Responsibility, too? That changes everything.

(The ship bell rings again.)

THE STRANGER
Do you hear, Ellida? It has rung now for the last time. Come.

ELLIDA (turns towards him, looks firmly at him, and speaks in a resolute voice)
I shall never go with you after this!

THE STRANGER
You will not!

ELLIDA (clinging to WANGEL)
I shall never go away from you after this.

THE STRANGER

So it is over?

ELLIDA
Yes. Over for all time.

THE STRANGER
I see. There is something here stronger than my will.

ELLIDA
Your will has not a shadow of power over me any longer. To me you are as one dead – who has come home from the sea, and who returns to it again. I no longer dread you. And I am no longer drawn to you.

THE STRANGER
Goodbye, Mrs. Wangel! (He swings himself over the fence.) Henceforth, you are nothing but a shipwreck in my life that I have tided over. (He goes out.)

WANGEL (looks at her for a while)
Ellida, your mind is like the sea – it has ebb and flow. Whence came the change?

ELLIDA
Ah! Don't you understand that the change came – was bound to come when I could choose in freedom?

WANGEL
And the unknown? – It no longer lures you?

ELLIDA
Neither lures nor frightens me. I could have seen it – gone out into it, if only I myself had willed it. I could have chosen it. And that is why I could also renounce it.

WANGEL
I begin to understand little by little. You think and conceive in pictures – in visible figures. Your longing and aching for the sea, your attraction towards this strange man, these were the expression of an awakening and growing desire for freedom; nothing else.

ELLIDA
I don't know about that. But you have been a good physician for me. You found, and you dared to use the right remedy – the only one that could help me.

50

WANGEL
Yes, in utmost need and danger we doctors dare much. And now you are coming back to me again, Ellida?

ELLIDA
Yes, dear, faithful Wangel – now I am coming back to you again. Now I can. For now I come to you freely, and on my own responsibility.

WANGEL (looks lovingly at her)
Ellida! Ellida! To think that now we can live wholly for one another –

ELLIDA
And with common memories. Yours, as well as mine.

WANGEL
Yes, indeed, dear.

ELLIDA
And for our children, Wangel?

WANGEL
You call them ours!

ELLIDA
They who are not mine yet, but whom I shall win.

WANGEL
Ours! (Gladly and quickly kisses her hands.) I cannot speak my thanks for those words! (Ibsen, 2001: n.p.)

In the Norwegian original text Ibsen in this scene uses the words '*frihet under ansvar*' (freedom '*under*' responsibility). In English translations this is usually rendered as the more common expression 'freedom on your own responsibility', which easily can be interpreted in the way that the only restriction on Ellida's freedom is the fact that she is the one responsible for whatever consequences her conduct may have for herself: she cannot blame others. But when Ibsen here uses the words 'freedom *under* responsibility' and especially in the context given in this scene, there can be no doubt that he means more than being responsible for consequences to oneself: my freedom is also restricted by my responsibility for the other(s). Ellida's decision to stay with her husband was voluntary, as she demanded from him that it should be (this time), but it was at the same time, as he appealed to her, a decision taken in a freedom emerging from her responsibility, not only towards herself and her own life, that is, not a freedom from responsibility (a freedom that Ibsen lets the stranger represent), but instead a decision made as a response to responsibility *for the other*, that is, for her husband and his children, her stepchildren.

This semantic change from the original Norwegian text to the English translation may also be interpreted as symptomatic for what has happened to the concept of freedom during the years between 1888 and now, and maybe even more as an illustration of the difference between a European continental and Anglo-American understanding of freedom. With his 'freedom *under* responsibility' Ibsen here clearly represents a Kantian, and by that a continental, view on individual freedom, where it is assumed that the moral law, and with it the responsibility for the other, is prior to laws and rights, while the common English translation may reflect the economic concept of freedom which, in contrast to continental, Kantian philosophy is better suited to Anglo-American, utilitarian ethics where freedom means primarily freedom *from* responsibility, in the sense that the individual only needs to take account of the consequences his or her choice may have for him or herself; such as, for instance, any sanctions from society, being from the market, the legal system or other social institutions established with the purpose of liberating individuals from their responsibility for the other. Kant, and Ibsen, on the other hand, will claim that such social mechanisms can never free us from our responsibility for the other, as this responsibility is embedded in us initially, prior to both individual freedom and social institutions.

ETHICS

5

Ethics of Care

An example

Let me now go back to the example from the introduction of chapter 3: Imagine that you are the financial manager of a hospital. The director has asked you to set up a proposal for a new budget for the hospital where expenditures have to be cut by a considerable amount of money compared to the current situation. In your proposal the nurses on several of the units of the hospital will be forced to work more efficiently, with fewer employees on duty at one time with the same number of patients. You have checked that this personnel reduction is possible within existing rules and national standards of what is medically defensible. The nursing personnel at several units, however, react vigorously to your proposal, as based on their professional and human considerations it will be ethically unjustifiable to the patients and their relatives.

The head of the nurses in one of the units feels completely powerless when she is presented with the decision and the arguments from management. Her professional knowledge as a nurse is based on care for the patients. When you, as the financial manager of the hospital, have a quite different, and apparently 'objective' view, it seems impossible for her to get anywhere with her arguments. Even if much of her professional knowledge of nursing about what is good for the patients and the involvement of their relatives is regarded as 'evidence-based', this is of little help to her against the arguments of the financial manager that budgets have to be held. Her professional knowledge rests ultimately on an ethical condition, which is good care for the patients, a condition which, compared with 'objective' economic facts, is considered subjective.

The general and the particular

The occasion in the above example was a requirement of the hospital management for expenditure cuts, a requirement that to the nurses appeared ethically indefensible towards the patients and their relatives. This example describes one of several similar confrontations between two different perspectives both within and outside work-life: on the one hand, knowledge about general and economic relations, and, on the other, knowledge from experience with particular single events. In such confrontations the general perspective will usually come out stronger than the particular one, because it has language and logic on its side and with that also the definitions of what *is*. In special cases, however, the particular and unique may 'break through'. Not only in hospital units but other places as well, also outside work life, a care is provided to others that cannot be explained by any kind of objective rationality, but that still everyone has experienced – and experiences daily – both as giver and receiver. These are occasions where the one giving care sets the other before himself or herself. These are not the cases where, based on instrumental knowledge, it is 'smart' to set the other first, as this will in the long run be to the best for oneself. The cases we are treating here are situations where one sets the other before oneself without reflecting upon it. Examples may be the nurse who, confronted with the needs of her patient, prioritises these before her own needs; it may be the teacher who prioritises the needs of her pupil before her own, and it could be the saleswoman who sets the needs of the customer before her own, not because she is told to do it by management, but as an immediate response to the encounter with her customer (for simplicity of expression I choose to refer to these professionals as 'she'). This need to provide care for others may to some even be a motivation to go into the profession. Other reasons for joining several of these professions, and staying there, with high work pressure and not a very high salary compared to those of others even within the same organization, may be hard to find.

If this providing of care, as it is described above, cannot be explained rationally in any way, it can still be described, without a logical and self-explaining structure, as we have earlier seen is the case with instrumental knowledge. When we in the following want to describe ethics as an idea, it must be an idea that is not self-centred from the outset, but instead an idea proposing that it is possible to set the other first, not as a conclusion of some logical chain of thought, but instead as an alternative point of departure.

In the professional ethics taught in health education this is already an established issue. The need for a more systematised ethics in these professions arises normally when one as a health worker is confronted with dilemmas caused by the impossibility of meeting the needs of everyone. In other words: professional ethics are developed from, among other things, experiences with what I here will call encounters with *the third*. At the moment the health worker is confronted with more than one who needs care – and sooner or later (rather sooner) he or she will – the health worker is forced to reflect, estimate and prioritise. This is often experienced – and described – as an ethical dilemma, because the encounter with each single other calls forth a responsibility to the health worker. This means that there is an ethics *before* the dilemma of professional ethics, dealing with what happens in the encounter with *the other*. This issue is treated by several authors, who are frequently referred to in the literature of professional ethics. Among these are Martin Buber, Emmanuel Levinas and Knud E. Løgstrup, who all three in different ways have expressed that being a human implies to relate to *the other*. To Buber (1987), being human is to enter the phenomenon of the *I-Thou*, as opposed to an *I-it*. To go into the *I-Thou* is a daring deed; one can never know what will come out of it; it is a risk that is connected to personal development. To Levinas (who will be presented in more detail in the next chapter), being human implies being an *I-for-the-Other*: having encountered the Other, I am, with all my knowledge, logic and predictability – all that makes me be me in the eyes of others – questioned. To Løgstrup (1997), a basic condition of being human is being 'intertwined' with the life of the other. From this fact I will always have a part of the other's life in my hands, and from there follows the ethical demand to take care of the other.

The personal experience of being confronted with the needs of the other gives rise to an ethical orientation that forms the base of professional knowledge – before any theoretical considerations are brought in, whether they are within ethics or economics. This ethical base may, however, come into conflict with a management perspective, which is, as we have seen, self-centred. For instance, there is an obvious difference concerning motivation: in health and social professions, the drive towards helping others may be the most important factor of motivation, while in management thinking the main factor of motivation is economic gain for the individual employee. In the next chapter I will show how Levinas' analysis of the encounter with *the third* can create a connection between these two factors of motivation, that is, between the ethical demand in the encounter with the other and the requirements of the economic system.

Ethics of care

In her book *Care*, with the subtitle *A Feminine Approach to Ethics and Moral Education*, Nel Noddings (1984) describes a mother's care for her child as an initiating experience for the development of ethics. To her, care for one's child is in the beginning not a question of morality or ethics; it is something inborn and natural. Morality comes later, and after that comes ethics, but they are both developed, according to Noddings, from natural care. A significant difference between this ethics of care and other, 'conventional' theories of ethics, is that while the traditional theories (such as those related to Kant, utilitarianism, etc.) start with autonomous individuals, the ethics of care starts with the *relation* between two persons, such as mother and child, or nurse and patient – in other words: between a care giver and a care receiver. The individual is defined by the relation: one becomes an individual through being in relations with others.

Noddings emphasises further that the source of ethics is non-rational. Here she refers to, among others, the child psychologist Urie Bronfenbrenner, who claimed that if children are to be able to develop, they will need a continuous irrational engagement from one or more adults in care and interaction. When Bronbenbrenner once was asked what he meant by 'irrational', he answered: "Somebody has got to be crazy about that kid!" (Noddings, 1984: 61).

Noddings claims that ethics develops from care, and in her argumentation she exemplifies this describing a specific case (1984: 82-84): when she as a mother wakes up at night from her infant's crying, she gets up and does what she can for the child. This is not a moral choice; it is a quite natural reaction. A mother who neglects the needs of her child is not considered immoral, but rather sick or in a situation that makes her unable to function normally as a mother. To feed an infant, as a response to its expressions of hunger, is an impulse we share with animals. Noddings claims that this impulse to provide care develops

58

further in humans towards what we call 'morality'. This implies that we do have a choice, but that to give care in such situations is more natural than not to give care. Not to give care to a person who expresses a need for it demands an explicit reason. It demands that one either deliberately denies a sense of belonging, or that one is deliberately changing an ethical standard, for instance out of some logic or rational reason. In this way we may say that the care a mother gives her infant, out of an inborn impulse, is the beginning of not only a more general care between people, but also a beginning of our ideas of what good and bad acts are between people, that is, morality, and by that, those reflections we make on morality, in other words what we call 'ethics'. Thus, caring for the other comes first, before any rules and principles.

Nodding says that the person who gives care is 'obsessed' by the other. To her, my care for the other comes before my own freedom. The freedom of the individual is thus conditioned by restrictions imposed by the other. Further, these restrictions on my freedom exist before, and not after, freedom itself is defined.

Ethical dilemmas

Nel Noddings is not the only author who has used the term 'ethics of care'. As we have already mentioned, the ethics of care starts with the relation, and not the individual, as the basic building block in describing how people think, feel and act. One problem with this kind of ethics, based on the relation to the other, is that there is also a third, a fourth, etc., and as soon as I am forced to relate to these as well, I will become uncertain when it comes to what an ethics of care demands of my responsibility for the other. And in addition: shouldn't I also take care of myself? Let us pursue this question one step further: an ethics of care has no way to deal with economic, administrative and organizational systems, where several considerations have to be made, not only ethical ones, but also ones regarding institutional procedures and inertness as well as man's limited ability to think and act rationally. In the 'brutal' confrontations with both the third and with the economy, ethical dilemmas easily arise. In the field of professional ethics much attention is paid to training in how to cope with ethical dilemmas. Without such training one may easily, when facing an ethical dilemma, end up in despair, cynicism or moralism, neither of which can be regarded as ethical.

Going back to the example of the meeting between the nurse and the financial manager, everyone will, and so must also the two parts involved, admit – after some reflection on the matter – that they are both right, from each of their subjective perspectives. Both have legitimate arguments for their claims, each from their position. But how can they both be right, and where can the situation move from there? Let us discuss this further by using the two concepts *mercy* and *justice*. 'Mercy' is a word we use as a substitute for a logical reason of a unilateral good act that does not expect any return. Care given by mercy needs no reason. When we show mercy to the other we do it as a singular case. The other is not in a position of deserving it, maybe rather the opposite: I may choose to show mercy instead of what from a justice point of view rather should require revenge or punishment. 'Justice', on the other hand, is the art of treating people equally, also in distribution of care and goods, independent of the person, only dependent on the situation, in the way that any other person in the same situation would have received the same treatment. Care given out of consideration for justice needs a reason. In this discussion I may use terms I have used earlier. Explaining *justice* belongs to the 'exercise' consisting of making singular situations equal to each other; it is rendering *the other* into *the same*, to the general, preferably by referring to universal principles. This is the exercise of language, which we also use when we define something by putting it into categories. *Acts of mercy*, on the other hand, belong to singular cases, the particularities that are not captured by generalising language and its logic. (That may also be why principles of mercy so easily turn into hypocrisy). In the meeting between the nurse and the financial manager the latter can explain and justify the expenditure cuts by claiming that he or she is responsible for *justice* in the allocation of resources available to the hospital. The nurse, on his or her side, will, from his or her encounter with the patient, and his or her own professional ethics, argue for *mercy* towards those who will suffer from the budget cuts. In that way mercy will come into conflict with justice, a conflict that will be thoroughly discussed in the next chapter. But, as I have already noted, justice has the power on its side, because it can be expressed in a general language, abstracted from the particular cases. The financial manager can easily refer to other particular cases, on other units of the hospital, where appeal is also made to mercy, but a mercy for others than those whom the nurse meets.

This conflict exemplifies what ethical dilemmas usually are about, in various versions of professional ethics. Going back to the ethics of care we will find no general solutions to these ethical dilemmas. The result is often a communication barrier between ethics of care on the one side and economic knowledge on the other. In the next chapter I will demonstrate how Levinas suggests a way to break through this barrier of communication. One of his points is to distinguish between the asymmetric encounter with the (different) other, on the one hand, and the symmetric meeting between several persons, out in society, in organizations and the economy, on the other. This makes Levinas especially suitable for understanding the relation between economy and ethics. More explicitly than other authors, Levinas insists that the transformation from relating to one other to that of relating to several others is not a continuous transition, but is instead a discontinuous jump. All 'good' experiences with another person, that is, all the ethical qualities such as trust, charity, love and respect, cannot immediately be transferred to relations to more than one other, that is, to the participation in economic and social reality. Instead they must be transformed through, for instance, the concept of *justice*. There is thus a crucial connection here: considering justice as something impersonal and exclusively rational is insufficient. However, if we want to apply ethics by finding just solutions to specific problems and dilemmas, Levinas' main contribution – that is, his discussion of the encounter with the Other – is not a part of such an 'applied ethics'. His concern was primarily to find the *meaning of ethics*. He asked, and tried to answer, the question 'Why do we strive for justice?' (when we do). But then it emerges, fortunately for us, that the answer he suggests to this question also helps us, both in finding a meaningful, general connection between mercy and justice, and in giving us an understanding of the economy and the monetary system as possible efficient means for justice – and also for injustice. This is the matter I shall now go into.

6

Ethics in the Economy

Emmanuel Levinas: a brief biography

In this chapter I will show how Levinas manages to connect ethics with economy. Before going into this, however, it may be useful to have a short review of his life and works.

Emmanuel Levinas was born in 1906 in the town Kaunas in Lithuania, which was then a part of Russia, neighbouring the region Kaliningrad, where another Emmanuel, Immanuel Kant, was born almost 200 years earlier. Levinas followed Kant's philosophy a long way, but his Jewish background and especially his experiences from the Second World War meant that Levinas did not follow Kant's and his Age of Enlightenment's optimism regarding the development of humanity. At the age of 17 Levinas went to Strasbourg in France to study philosophy. In 1931 he became a French citizen and he regarded himself as French, living in Paris for the rest of his life. During the holocaust his entire family in Lithuania was killed and he later said that his biography "is dominated by a presentiment of the Nazi terror and its memory thereafter" (Levinas, 1990: 291). Parallel to his philosophical production Levinas published a great number of interpretations of Jewish scriptures. Although he kept these two interests apart from each other, there is no doubt that his contribution to philosophy draws on the Jewish tradition. After the Holocaust Levinas lost any illusion he may have had that ethics develops from reason, as Kant suggested. Reason is based in the self while ethics comes to the self as a disturbing element in the encounter with the face of the Other. He agreed with Kant that the moral law comes before anything else, also before any attempts to put words to it, as something both universal and holy. As

63

opposed to Kant, however, Levinas meant that ethics cannot be captured by reason. He elaborates this idea in his first main work, *Totality and Infinity* (Levinas, 1991a), first published in 1961. Here he emphasises that what Kant called the moral law has its source outside the I, namely in the Other. In his second main work, first published in 1974, with the English title *Otherwise than Being, or, Beyond Essence* (Levinas, 1991b), he adjusted some of his views on the source of moral law. Ethics is found within the self, but is still inaccessible to reason. It can only be awakened and manifested as a response to the call for responsibility from the Other.

Levinas entered a dialogue with the French postmodern philosophers, especially with the most prominent of them, Jacques Derrida. This dialogue has given his philosophy resilience in confrontations with so-called 'deconstruction' in postmodern thinking. This is especially important to ethics: all Western philosophy from Aristotle to Kant (and, if one wishes, even further) appears to many as just empty words faced with all the cruelty and inhumanity we see in the world today. Levinas 'saves' the source of ethics exactly by lifting it out of a cruel reality, but without at the same time lifting it into any religious or ethical domain. This will be further explained in the following.

The conatus

"Each thing in so far as it is in itself endeavours to persist in its own being". This is one of the basic propositions of Spinoza's *Ethics* (1997: 98). It applies to all unliving, such as a stone, and it applies to all living, such as a human. It can be applied also to physical and biological systems. The human body is composed of cells possessing as their most important aspect a 'drive' to continue to exist; they have through evolution developed the ability to maintain both themselves and the part of their environment on which they depend to keep living, that is, other cells, and their 'host', the body. Thus, the body does what 'it' can to continue to be. Spinoza's proposition may also be applied to the human as a mental being (neurophysiologists will certainly see a connection here): *I will continue to be me*. This will to preserve oneself Spinoza called (in Latin) *conatus essendi*.

Violence and murder are to Levinas (1985: 86) extreme cases of the *conatus*. The need for economic freedom and the economic knowledge supporting this need is also an implication of the conatus. But Spinoza's idea of a large 'we' as an all-encompassing, harmonious deity is not found in the works of Levinas, and this became even clearer to Levinas after the Holocaust. According to Zygmunt Bauman (1989) the Holocaust was a natural consequence of modernity. The time was mature when it became technologically and organizationally possible. Levinas went deeper: the Holocaust was an expression of the human *conatus*.

In his struggle for freedom, autonomy and happiness, man has to – as I have described earlier in this book – *conceive* his surroundings, including his fellow men. In my own 'project of being', consisting primarily in obtaining and exercising individual freedom and achieving a good life, I also involve others. This project is driven by a will to 'totalise' the world, within a conceivable knowledge. Economic freedom presumes a self-centred understanding of reality (Burggraeve, 2003: 57).

Business ethics, in the sense of ethics *for* business, illustrates this: its perspective is that of an 'enlightened self-interest' where the constraints that are put on the individual, thanks to the ability to see the unfortunate consequences for oneself, postpone the 'war', in a direct or metaphoric sense of the word (*ibid.*: 70-71). This enlightened self-interest forms the base not only of the market economy, but also of a social organization and manifestation of human rights, and even of some ethical theories. It is a calculated and voluntary renunciation of one's own freedom in order to obtain in return security and other common goals (*ibid.*: 72).

The fact that economic, political and legal theories appeal to enlightened self-interest does not imply, however, that we should discard them. Nor should we reject proclamations of human rights, legal constraints of individual freedom and, for that matter, business ethics, even if they are based on an enlightened self-interest. It is rather the opposite: such institutions and knowledge are indispensable because the primary quality of the enlightened self-interest is that it restricts egocentricity. Our *practical reason* (which was Kant's words for the reason that governs our acts, where the moral law is embedded as a principle) includes the knowledge that it can be rational to lay certain restrictions on individual freedom. In this way practical reason may postpone (for an indefinite time) violence and murder among people. This has primarily been the *raison-d'être* of politics and the state, but it is today taken over more and more by corporate organizations, as expressed in the new term for business ethics, as *corporate social responsibility* and *corporate citizenship* (see chapter 2). Thanks to this 'postponement of violence' provided by politics and economic rationality, people may unfold their freedom within the laws and regulations set up by society (Burggraeve, 2003: 77).

Beyond this observation, however, and more interestingly to Levinas – and to us – is the question from where the idea derives that there is a possible alternative to pursuing one's self-interest, enlightened or not. Levinas' answer to this question is that this idea is called forth in me in the encounter with the different other, who denies to be captured by me and my understanding.

The call of the Other

All instrumental knowledge, such as business management, is, and has to be, as already noted, normative, conventional and logically explainable. But there are also other motives for our actions, which are neither normative, conventional nor explainable (as these properties are explained in the previous chapter), as we discover when the subject sets itself aside to the advantage of the other (and when this is not calculated, as in an 'enlightened self-interest'), for instance in a mother's care for her child or a nurse's care for his or her patient. Within a rational frame of understanding this kind of inexplicable behaviour is often made invisible, as it lacks linguistic and understandable categories.

The motive for these actions of setting the other before oneself is what I here call *ethics*. A possible explanation of why ethics, as an idea of the good, may emerge is the following: a human has the faculty to be conscious and to reflect about himself or herself. Thus he or she can also observe his or her own *conatus*, and he or she has the possibility to question this *conatus*. By the same faculty the I can also question itself as a subject, driven by its *conatus*. The ability of questioning oneself and one's *conatus* is called forth in the presence of the Other, as a response to the call of the Other. But Levinas goes even further than this: neither the I nor its *conatus* exists by itself before the Other enters the scene. The manifestation of the I and the manifestation of the *conatus* is a response to the call of the Other. The Other is 'there' before the I; in fact, the I is formed as a result of responses and interaction, starting with the Other addressing the becoming I. Further, the call of the Other can only be responded to by the I by standing up and saying (explicitly or implicitly) 'here I am', that is, by taking responsibility as a responsible I. Only when the I has announced itself as a responsible I, can the development of the self and the development of its knowledge, and with this a common understanding of the world, proceed.

As a consequence of the assumption that the call for responsibility from the Other is prior to my understanding of the world, the Other cannot be included in this understanding. The Other remains unintelligible to me, in the sense that it is impossible for me to put him or her in a category without reducing him or her into the same as something else, and thus reducing him or her into an object, within my concept and my language, and thereby causing a violation of him or her as a unique person. To be confronted with the non-understandable is an experience that invites me to think, at the same time as it escapes thought. The impossibility of understanding the Other is exactly what makes me realise that not everything can be captured by my concepts and understanding (Burggraeve, 2003: 91). This experience invites me to humility in my approach to others.

As the reader will have noticed already, it has been common in English translations of the works of Levinas to write 'the Other' with a capital 'O'. This notation underlines the point that the other person cannot be controlled by denoting it in a category through a word; he or she remains a unique person, a respect we also show when writing names with capital initials.

Ethics, defined as the idea that it is possible to do otherwise than setting oneself before others, presumes an ability to be open towards the Other without the intention to fully understand. To the subject the Other is objectively given because he or she is there regardless of whether or not the subject is there. The Other meets me with his or her *face*. The face is that which addresses me and calls for a response. It questions me, the fact that I am, and the fact that in my own self-centredness I make efforts to preserve my own being. The face of the Other questions me, without any language, what right I have to be and whether I, simply by being, take the place of someone else (Levinas, 1985: 121).

The face of the Other is unthematisable, but still Levinas again and again tries to approach it verbally. This may seem to be a paradox, which Levinas admits. One way of describing this paradox is to say that from my encounter with the (unthematisable) face of the Other I am brought into social reality with other people (the third, the fourth, etc., including the reader) and in this world I can use language to describe the encounter with the Other from an immemorable past.

One of several of Levinas' descriptions of the face of the Other is to call it vulnerable and naked, as it cannot hide itself behind something that represents it. At the same time it offers itself to me, because it has no other way to communicate than by its appearance. To me the encounter with the Other comes in conflict with my need to understand and explain, a need that is at the base of my efforts to exist as an I, a need that is also the root of violence against others. To me, with my *conatus*, the face of the Other, through its weakness and vulnerability, creates a temptation and a challenge to exert violence (Levinas, 1985: 86). The naked and mortal face invites me and my *conatus* to reduce it to something I can control, so that I can eliminate the non-understandable. This is why Levinas can say that the *conatus* is a response to the call of the Other. But at the same time, by its mere appearance, the face also resists being controlled by me (Burggraeve, 2003: 96-97). The face of the Other appears to me as a disarming authority.

My *conatus* and my efforts to understand the world develop from a response to the call from the Other, while the Other remains inaccessible to these efforts. The Other's call for responsibility comes to me in spite of my self, my *conatus* and my knowledge. This experience contradicts how I understand my own place in my own understanding of the world. As the Copernican revolution followed from the discovery that the earth was not the centre of the Universe, Levinas insists that the thinking subject is not at the centre of its own universe. It is no longer I who acknowledges and estimates the other; prior to that it is I who am evaluated, acknowledged, estimated, and questioned (Levinas, 1991b: 109). This substitution with regards to who is in the centre of my universe is not something I can decide. It is not the free subject who actively gives place to the Other (or chooses not to do so). The centre of my universe is already, before I can do anything as a subject, occupied by the Other, as the one who addresses me and by that 'awakens' my self (*ibid.*: 99-102).

The Copernican revolution did not only explain why the earth is not the centre of the universe; it also explained why and how, seen from the earth, it looks like the earth still is at the centre. (The new knowledge emerged exactly because there was something wrong with this presupposition). Similarly, we can say that Levinas describes the self-centredness and its important and indispensable role in all instrumental knowledge, but at the same time also the 'discovery' that there is something that cannot be right in this conventional, self-centred knowledge: if the self-centredness had not been continuously questioned by the Other we would have had an ever escalating process of conflicts ending in violence and murder.

I cannot choose not to respond to the call of the Other. I cannot escape the appeal in the face of the Other. I have to respond. *How* I respond will depend on how I use my freedom, but all that I choose to say and to do is a response to the Other addressing me. An attempt to ignore the Other is, morally, a strongly negative response; it is an attempt to reduce the Other to an object. The face of the Other calls me to respond 'yes', that is, 'here I am', but I can say 'no' by pretending I am invisible. But what I then actually do is to pretend that the Other is invisible, which is a violation of him or her. (The context may of course be such that there is a common acceptance that one cannot greet everyone, as for instance in a big city. Such conventions are parts of the social constructions that necessarily have to follow from the meeting with the third, which will be discussed soon). The face confronts me with the choice of either turning the Other into an object and a means in my *conatus*, or committing myself to the (unconditioned) call for responsibility.

The striving for justice

What is original in Levinas compared to other authors who also have defined being a human as being related to another human, such as, for instance, Buber and Løgstrup (mentioned in the previous chapter), and those representing the ethics of care (also presented in the previous chapter), is that Levinas acknowledges that I not only meet the Other, but also *the third*, as the Other. By meeting the third I am again confronted with an appeal for mercy. From this – as a result of an intention of being responsible – I am forced to evaluate, compare, reason and to seek what is *just*. Justice exerts violence but is still better than injustice. In my efforts towards more justice I must compare, and in this comparing I may have to count, also money; it may even be necessary to set a price for a human life, something that, from the point of view of mercy, is a scandal, but still necessary, because the third is also there. It is necessary to count; the question is why I count. Is it out of my *conatus*, which, if it is allowed to unfold freely without being questioned (or, alternatively, if I ignore the questioning), will lead to violence? Or is it out of mercy, which comes to me as an imperative in the encounter with the Other, and which, in the encounter with the third – as the Other – drives me to seek always more justice? This is not only about counting, it is about being in general – why and how I am. Levinas will insist that "To be or not to be, that is *not* the question" (Cohen in Levinas, 1985: 10). Instead, it is a question of *how* I am a being together with others in the world. Ethics comes before ontology.

An objection to Noddings' ethics of care is that the mother-infant-situation is not a common one. It is instead a special situation where special qualities are called forth, that are not found elsewhere in society. To believe that the good is natural can be naïve; it can even be dangerous. Looking around in the world today the opposite would be more natural to claim: we have a natural inclination towards controlling and reducing the Other, with violence, physical or psychological. But through the encounter with the Other we are told that this is wrong. It is this small 'source of the good' which dominates a mother when she is alone with her infant.

At the moment we have to relate to more than one other we understand that we need to make some efforts to understand the situation of the other individuals, their special situations and needs, so that we can know what is just in our dealing with others. It is his discussion of the meeting with the third that makes Levinas' philosophy so relevant to economy, although most presentations of his philosophy concentrate on the encounter with the Other, and may thus cause the misunderstanding that this is his ethics, and consequently a quite impossible one. However, as mentioned earlier, Levinas' description of the encounter with the Other is his answer to the question of what is the meaning of ethics, or, why we at all (at least sometimes) want justice. In short, to Levinas, the task of the economy is to contribute to justice. The cause of the striving for justice is the imperative of mercy in the encounter with the Other. And as there is always more than one other my experience of the encounter with the Other cannot be directly transferred to social reality. I must perform a brutal transformation from mercy to justice (but which nevertheless is less brutal than me not caring about justice), and in doing so I need as much as I can possibly acquire of what is available of detailed knowledge of each particular situation, as well as my ability to reason logically.

It is not only a fact that ethics is necessary for the economy. Economy is also necessary for ethics. Just as a house may be a concrete security for a loan, the economy is a concrete security for ethics. Without economic goods and needs and the accompanying knowledge *for myself*, there would have been no need for ethics. An ethics *for the other* can only be expressed as long as the other has specific needs competing with mine. Only then can I act for the other *instead of* acting for myself, and thus set the needs of the other before those of me. Or, put in another way: angels do not need ethics, because they have no needs and thus no need to help each other.

Levinas on the role of money

In his article 'Sociality and money', based on a speech given in 1986 to the Belgian Association of Saving Banks, Levinas suggests that the call for mercy is transformed into a striving for justice in a monetary society. Below is the last and summing up paragraph of this article, interrupted with my comments:

> The third, other than the neighbour, is also my neighbour and my neighbour's neighbour. (Levinas, 2007: 206)

Levinas addresses here an issue that is often neglected in ethical literature: I face not only one other person, but other others as well. This question is crucial with respect to economic life. Levinas has been criticised for not having dealt properly with more than one other. I do not agree with this criticism. On the contrary, Levinas emphasises the necessity of going from the Other to the third, as will be clearly shown in the following.

> Are the elevation and sanctity of love for the neighbour not comprised in this lack of concern for the third which, in an anonymous totality, can have been the victim of that very one I answer for and that I approach in the mercy and charity of dis-inter-estedness? (*ibid.*)

Here Levinas indicates how the ethical dilemma generated by my encounter with both the Other and the third is approached: the encounter with the Other in which I am called to show mercy does not belong to the social inter-being (*inter-est*) of men and women, that is, where I also encounter the third (and the fourth etc). Instead, the encounter with the Other is *detached from this inter-being* (*dis-inter-ested*). In

71

this encounter with the Other, detached from social inter-being, I may also meet the third, but then as the Other. Actually, it may very well be that it is the third whom I encounter in this way, as it is the third who easily becomes the victim of my mercy and charity towards the Other.

> Between the unique ones, a comparison, a judgement is needed. Justice is needed in the very name of their dignity as unique and incomparable. (*ibid.*)

Here Levinas introduces the problem of comparison and justice. Each person I meet is unique, but as I am confronted with more than one other, I am forced to compare and to judge between them. This is a violation in itself. On the other hand, however, the very idea of justice in such comparisons and judgements has its source in my encounter with the one, unique Other, in the dignity and incomparability which follows from the uniqueness of this Other. The idea of justice is thus an idea of minimising the necessary violation caused by my placing the third second when I place the Other first. Consequently, no solution can ever be just enough.

But how then can I obtain the most just solution possible between more than one other? To this question Levinas now turns:

> But to compare the incomparable is, undoubtedly, to approach people by returning to the totality of men in the economic order, in which their acts are measured in the homogeneity immanent to money, without being absorbed or simply added up in this totality. (*ibid.*)

My encounter with the Other is, as already mentioned, detached from the social inter-being of men and women. This does not mean that my encounter with the Other takes place in a separate, exclusive space where I am alone with the Other, sheltered from the rest of the world. When I encounter the face of the Other I am at the same time placed in social and economic reality with the third. And it is exactly the economic order, with money as a homogenous measure of value, that provides me with what I need in order to be able to compare and to seek justice in my comparing, in my judging and my use of rational tools such as budgets, so that my violation of the third can become as small as possible. It is because my encounter with the Other takes place in the midst of social and economic reality, and not in some separated, other place, that I am continuously reminded that the third is also the Other, a reminder that helps me to avoid the third disappearing as a number in a row within the social and economic system.

> The saintliness of the human rising above being persevering in its being, and above the violences this perseverance perpetuates, heralds response, in mercy and charity, to the face of the Other; but it also appeals to Reason and law. (*ibid.*)

The being and the inter-being of men and women is dominated by 'persevering in being' and by the violation of others caused by this perseverance. However, elevated above this inter-being I am confronted with, in the face of the Other, the saintliness of the human. The face of the Other appeals to my mercy. But as the third is also the Other, the face of the Other also calls me to seek, through reason and through law, always more justice.

> However, justice already requires a State, institutions, rigour and an informed and impartial authority. But an already liberal State capable of better legislation. (*ibid.*)

Striving for justice requires states and organizations with all that follows from these forms of consistency and authority. But because no social and economic system can ever be just enough, organizations must be liberal, in the sense that they are prepared to review their own rules, and to reopen previous cases, towards always more justice.

> And consciences awoken in their uniqueness to unpredictable resources to which an ever harsh universality can bring non-deducible grace. (*ibid.*)

Levinas closes the text by reminding us that the unforeseeable and the undeserved of mercy towards my neighbour should not be kept out of social and economic reality. Humanity and charity come into the world as 'non-deducible grace', as for instance when I as a leader am forced to compare the incomparable of each of my employees, in distributing a limited budget among them. Then I must at the same time see each of them as unique individuals, not only in order to be reminded to seek as much justice as possible (by means of reason and correct calculations), but also so that I can show mercy to any one of them, when an unforeseen opportunity for this suddenly emerges.

Summing up Levinas

When I as a *being* do what I can to persist in being, I follow what Spinoza calls the *conatus* of all beings, dead or alive. In this *conatus* I am basically self-centred (with the reservations I will soon make); all I think and do, including my ability and my efforts to understand, or conceive, the world around me, has a self-centred perspective – it is *I* who conceives *my* surroundings – as well as a self-centred goal – it is *I* who is to persist. In this way Levinas explains our behaviour in the market, which is to seek welfare and happiness for ourselves. (But we also seek welfare and happiness for others; see below.) In this way he also explains Nazism, as well as the inclination to violence and murder throughout the history of man. (But not even Nazis were without ethics – again: stay with me to the next link in my line of arguments).

But – and this is what I have denoted 'the call of the Other' – humans have as the only beings (as far as we know) the faculty to be conscious about themselves. This means that I can reflect upon my own *conatus*, and thus question it. I am able to acknowledge that the *conatus* is not a natural law, but that it is also possible for me not to follow it. But why should I want to do otherwise than pursue my self-interest? And what should that be? By help of my own self-consciousness I can only grasp the idea that it is possible to do otherwise than to follow my *conatus*. Which other, meaningful possibilities there could be will not become clear to me until I meet the Other, that is, another human being. Meeting the Other, with his or her needs, I realise that it is possible for me to be *for the Other*. But I can, of course, choose whether I at all want to do anything for the Other, or if I will still prioritise myself, that is, follow my *conatus*. In other words, the *conatus* is no longer a given instinct, it is a response to the call for responsibility from the Other. With acknowledging the possibility of prioritising the Other before myself, which it is up to me to choose or not, I 'discover' ethics as something that comes to me before any understanding, conception and concepts, and which exists independently of me and my conceived world.

But – and here is the background to what I have denoted 'the striving for justice' – life is not as simple as having a choice between only two alternatives: either to pursue my self-interest, that is, to prioritise myself before the Other, or to follow the ethical appeal to prioritise the Other before myself. I cannot only relate to only one other; I will continuously meet more than one other. Thus I must also decide how to prioritise between them. Levinas suggests a way of how this is actually done in society. As already mentioned, his point was to view ethics as a possibility, namely the possibility to break with the self-centred *conatus*, that is, the possibility to set the Other before oneself. He certainly speaks about an ethical demand in the encounter with the Other as an imperative to be unconditionally for the Other, and not as some type of half-hearted request to also think of the Other. But it is nevertheless still up to me to decide whether I will meet this demand. The only thing I know for certain is that I am also responsible for whatever I choose to do. Thus, even if I can choose my own actions I cannot choose away the responsibility, neither for my actions nor for not acting. It is this possibility to choose that makes it possible to discuss ethics at all; if we had acted out of necessity there would have been no ethics. Out in society, among other people, ethically, it is the *possibilities* that are of importance, more than what becomes the outcome in each singular case. I may prioritise myself before all others, as, for instance, in my market behaviour, or in an exertion of violence. But there is also another possibility and that is, as I have already pointed out, something I realise when confronted with the Other, who questions me and thus makes me able to set the Other before myself. Among more than one other, however, I can no longer set the Other first without at the same time de-prioritising all the other others. In an ethical perspective the meeting with several others thus becomes the meeting with a brutal reality: to put one other first is to put all others behind. Meeting the other others implies an unavoidable violence, Levinas says, because by prioritising the Other I de-prioritise the third. Therefore, putting the Other first can be an ethical act only in the encounter with one other. Thus, the encounter with the Other, in the way Levinas describes it, does not belong to 'this world', as there is also the third. Nevertheless, Levinas describes the encounter with the Other as a human experience, as a phenomenon, described in the phenomenological tradition, as it appears to the subject.

In society, in the economy, in an organization, in short, in any social reality, to put one other first would not be a good moral act, as it implies ignoring the third. Ethics, in the special sense that I am first called to responsibility by the Other, has thus, to me, as a subject, meaning only in a particular event of encountering only one other. The meeting with the third and thereby with society in general, may thus easily lead me back to the self-centred conatus (interrupted only by sporadic encounters with the Other, maybe expressed as strong bonds of loyalty to one or a few like-minded others), because ethics in its original sense becomes impossible.

The idea behind this application of ethics is crucial to Levinas: the ethical appeal in the encounter with first the Other and then the third – also as the Other – makes me try to make my response to the third as little brutal as possible. This I can achieve by always striving for more justice – not for the sake of *the Other*, but for that of *the others*. To strive for always more justice does not mean to fight for one's own rights. Instead it means to make the transition from the experience of what it means to place the Other first, to the meeting with the third and the impossibility of placing the Other and the third first, with the least possible violence to all. The acknowledgement of the possibility of breaking with my conatus and of instead setting the Other first is thus the source of the wish for more justice; it is from the acknowledgement of the ethical possibility in the encounter with the Other that I find meaning in the desire for more justice in my responses to the *others*.

By acknowledging the necessity of the brutal transition from putting the Other first to justice, from the Other to all the other others, Levinas' philosophy becomes more realistic than many of those ethical theories that concentrate on my relation to the other without regard for the third, which is the problem with the ethics of care I discussed in the previous chapter. Levinas' philosophy has also become an important reference in so-called 'post-Holocaustian ethics', pursuing the discussion of what kind of ethics can be credible at all after the Holocaust, when all well-known ethical theories and ideals developed by and within Western 'civilisation' to still more people appear as nothing but 'empty words', without any consequences for people's lives. His philosophy does not end up with a certain ethical theory, presented as an addition to knowledge and its understanding of empirical reality. Instead, his conclusion is that we must *recur* to the practical, social and economic life and the existing empirical knowledge about it, or, as Husserl taught him – and us: we must go to 'the thing itself'. Only then will we realise that all people in their lives are driven by their *conatus* and a self-centred need to understand the world around them, but also by something more than that, or else we would have had no concepts of ethics. What we have learned from our short 'travel' out to this world and back again is that people have a desire for more justice and that we now know where this desire comes from: there is within us a desire for justice which does not come from any logical lines of reasoning saying that some justice may be 'smart' in the view of an enlightened self-interest, but which instead comes from:

1. My experiences of the encounter with the Other, making me realise that my *conatus* is one but not the only possible response to this encounter, another being to prioritise the Other before myself; and

2. Acknowledging that together with the others I have a possibility to make the necessary brutality against the third, who is also the Other, less brutal, by always striving for more justice, in the market, in society and within any kind of organization.

What is needed in order to find new and more just solutions and systems is first and foremost knowledge about these systems, that is, about markets and about production, performance and distribution of goods and services; it is this knowledge to which we will have to recur, instead of first rejecting it by declaring it exclusively immoral and then seeking some or other general, ethical theory.

It is a point of importance to describe the striving for more justice as an effort towards 'always more justice' and not 'continuously more justice'. This is because it cannot be taken for granted that even the very strongest efforts for achieving more justice will make society continuously more just. The *conatus*, when it unfolds in the market and in society at large, often works in the opposite direction, causing frequent setbacks with respect to justice, both locally, nationally and globally, as we may observe in political regimes where political support for free market forces replaces the substantial and useful knowledge (that may well be instrumental) about the industries, goods and services which it is all about. Thus, we have no guarantee that it will all 'end well'. In fact, we will never reach a society that is 'just enough'.

But if our efforts are sound in our recurrence to knowledge, in economics, political science, law, education, social work, medicine, nursing etc., together with our newly acquired insight in the aforementioned reason and desire for always more justice, and with certain possibilities to set this knowledge out in practice, it is still possible to hope.

Summary, Conclusion and Consequences

Summary

News media from time to time present stories of events where business leaders have 'passed the line' of what is considered to be decent. As discussed in the introduction of this book, it is not easy to know how common such cases are. It may also be that the appointment of a scapegoat belongs to a social-psychological mechanism, so that we all can preserve the belief that these events are exceptions from a general rule, suggesting that business leaders most of the time behave within both moral and legal boundaries. As soon as the scapegoat is removed, order and system are re-established, until the next event occurs. As one cannot exclude the possibility that such events may occur more frequently than we want to believe, I have in this book chosen a perspective on the relation between ethics and economy that may make it easier to approach such events: cases of 'misconduct' are actually easy to understand. Business leaders are under constant pressure to stretch limits in order to obtain always better results. It is the cases (how rare or frequent they may be) where they *resist* the temptation to make such decisions that need to be explained. From this perspective the following question would be the most natural to ask: from where comes the idea that it is possible to do otherwise than to place oneself before others? This idea, which I have called 'the idea of the good', is in this book what I have called *ethics*. The next question is then: how is this idea of the good put into practice? These two questions I have tried to answer in this book. Let me give a short summary of the discussion before I suggest my answers to them.

I started by describing economic thought and how it emerged in the Age of Enlightenment from the individual's desire for freedom. I then showed how economic knowledge in recent years has primarily changed from being knowledge for society and government authorities to becoming knowledge for the management of companies. As a natural extension of this 'new economic knowledge' the knowledge called 'business ethics' has developed to meet the demand of business leaders to know how to cope with ethical challenges made by society.

Then I discussed the phenomenon of subjectivity, especially related to the efforts of understanding. I showed how all understanding has a self-centred perspective, a property that does not call for moral criticism, but instead tells us that reason and understanding have their limits, particularly when it comes to approaches that we usually consider *ethical*.

From this preliminary conclusion I then moved to the part of reality where ethics actually is practiced, more specifically in the professions of care, and how an ethics of care is described within these professions. I showed how this ethics of care runs into a problem in its confrontation with 'economic reality', because it does not sufficiently treat the qualitative jump from relating to one other to that of relating to more than one other. From there I introduced the philosophy of Emmanuel Levinas, ending with his reflections on monetary society. In short, Levinas teaches us that through the encounter with the Other my self-centred *conatus* is questioned and thereby awakens the idea in me that it is possible to do otherwise than setting myself before others, not only as an idea, but as an ethical call. Such an appeal of putting the Other first in all situations, however, is impossible to live up to, as there is always more than one other who appeals to my mercy. The best I can do is to make the violations of the others less than they are, resulting in knowledge-based reflections on the concept of *justice*.

Instead of finishing with an ethical theory, or with a general theory of justice, Levinas concludes that we must recur to reality and the knowledge we have already acquired about this reality. Only knowledge about the real world can help us find the best options for making arrangements, routines or rules more just. There is already a lot of knowledge on justice; think only of all knowledge within the legal system and the field of law. One question, however, that is seldom asked within this knowledge is *why* we seek justice. Certainly, there have been attempts to explain this question logically and scientifically (and by that also self-centredly), by presenting justice as some sort of enlightened self-interest. But this still does not provide any sufficient explanation as to why we seek justice. The answer to this question, according to Levinas, cannot fully be explained in words, because the I as a thinking subject is 'set out of function' in the moment this insight reaches me, in the way that I and my being is questioned in the encounter with the Other. Ethics and thus also the proper meaning of justice is something I can only find in the face of the Other; it cannot be thematised further by my own concepts and my own understanding, as these tools can only be applied in a self-centred perspective.

Conclusion

In my introduction I posed the following two questions, to which this book has tried to develop answers:

1. From where does the idea that it is possible to do otherwise than privileging oneself over others come?

2. This idea, which we may call 'the idea of the good', or, as we will call it here, *ethics* – how is it transformed into practical conduct?

Based on the discussion in this book I will suggest the following answers to these questions:

1. The idea that there are other ways of acting than to choose those acts which set myself before others, in other words, the idea I have here called *ethics*, is not developed from reason. Instead, it strikes me as a disturbing idea in the direct encounter with another human being. But as I will always have to relate to more than this one Other, this idea of the good, of being an *I-for-the-Other*, is something that does not belong to the social world of inter-being among people. If it did, I would have favoured the *one other* before all *other others*. Ethics, as the idea of the good, will thus have to be transformed into something else before it can be applied in practice. This makes question 2 no less important than question 1.

2. The idea of the good, striking me in the encounter with the one Other, becomes a reason for me to endeavour to act justly and to always be more just, so that any violation of others can become less

than it is, through the necessary comparison, counting, evaluation and prioritising that I am always forced to make. At the same time it is important that the systems, rules and routines in which I take part in order to form and sustain them, as they can never become just enough, are given space also to show mercy towards each one, acts that may cause a change towards more justice from the existing routines, rules and systems.

Let us look a little closer at the implications of these answers. In the introduction to this book I chose the following perspective: the actions for which business leaders are criticised for showing bad social responsibility are actually easy to understand; it is their job to concentrate on the interests of their company and not on those of society. It is rather the cases where business leaders actually show responsibility beyond themselves and their own company that need to be explained. If the actions they are criticised for are the type of actions that prioritise their own individual interests, these may easily be understood as following on from the *conatus*. It is natural, not only for humans, but for all that exists, to do what is possible in order to continue to exist. In extreme cases this *conatus* may lead to violence and murder; in less extreme cases individuals try to control others through their use of language and through their understanding of reality, an understanding that will always have a self-centred perspective. What is often denoted as greed is an expression of the same *conatus* and should thus be easy to understand; expressions of the opposite may easily seem hypocritical. On the other hand, when business managers and other decision makers from time to time resist the temptation to follow this *conatus*, it is, according to Levinas, because, in the confrontation with another human being, they know that they have to answer for and explain their actions. When such a confrontation, or even only the thought of it, makes them choose otherwise than what simple business logic tells them, it is because the face of the Other has called forth the idea that such an alternative is possible, the idea we have here called *ethics*. However, as we have also seen, this idea cannot be put into practice as it is, because it does not belong to the social reality where I always have to relate to several others. The encounter with the Other takes place detached from this world, but it still works as a constant reason to act justly, in ways that attempt to make the violations of each of the others less than they are.

It is an important observation that this idea of the good does not always occur to the subject, nor that it always arouses attempts to find more just solutions. This is something we all know. What we can say to this is that in those cases where people actually choose differently to what is best for themselves, it may be because of ethics as an idea, as it is accounted for in this book, and what this idea leads to with regards to efforts toward justice, including our legal system as well as social institutions established to reduce injustice.

Let me also say something about this difficult point about the encounter with the Other as something that takes place 'not in the real world' of inter-being among people. There exists a considerable literature about leadership and co-operation emphasising the importance of care, relations and closeness in society and working life. Such approaches to organization and working life communicate an important and valuable insight about the ethical relations between employer and employee. But they have all the same limitation and thus the same problem, earlier described in chapter 5 about the ethics of care: the relation to the third is hardly or not at all discussed, other than in treating the third as the other as an ethical ideal. This is of little help in the encounter with 'economic reality'. To put the Other first will always be to the cost of the third. Such an ethics of care, closeness or relations treated by this literature will thus have the weakness that it may become a tool for the opposite purpose of what it recommends, that is, exclusion and violation of the third party standing outside the close relation. In this way 'regimes of goodness', trying to 'practice ethics', may become even worse than regimes based on the self-centred *conatus*, because the first have already 'taken care of' ethics, that is, in relation to each other, but excluding those who are outside the relationships. What is neglected in such 'regimes of goodness' is that the transformation from the Other to the third, that is, the transition from the one-to-one relation of a particular event to a social system with more than two participants and the general rules of this system, is not a continuous transition. It is rather the opposite: the transition from relating to only one to dealing with several others is discontinuous; it is a transition from mercy to justice, a transition that is brutal but necessary, when the ethical ideal meets economic reality.

It is said about good leaders that they are 'strict but just'. It should not be necessary to put in the 'but' in this expression: to be just *is* to be strict. But not only that: justice may sometimes be quite brutal from an ethical perspective, that is, against such ethical values as charity and mercy. If I should try to characterise a good leader, it should rather be to say that he or she is 'charitable but just', as it is the claim for justice that sets the limits to how much charity and care one can bring from the meeting with the one Other to the meeting with the third (and the fourth, etc.).

The slow, bureaucratic and centralistic economic systems were discarded by the people (both in West and East) mainly because they were regarded as unjust: first, they sustained unjust privileges for the top leaders and their relatives and, secondly, they caused a waste of resources. The discontent arose not because waste is wrong in itself (*consumption* is an example of economic waste that is not considered wrong), but because the waste was experienced as wrong because people did not receive goods that they could have received. In the same way the newer systems, following from an increased market orientation, such as introducing competition, privatisation and increased global trade, should be evaluated by how just they are. Are more resources spent on administration and high wages and privileges to leaders than what is considered just? Are those who receive welfare services that are now produced in competition better off than before? Is the gap between rich and poor becoming smaller? In other words, we should, as we have learned from Levinas, not remain in the ideal world of theories, but instead recur to reality.

Consequences

Having arrived at these conclusions the book would be incomplete if it stops here. Concluding that we should not remain in the spheres of theories but from there recur to reality, I am obliged to answer how that can be done. If the practical consequence of ethics, according to Levinas, are efforts towards always more justice, what does that mean? What consequences will this have for business and for politics? And what consequences will ethics in the sense of Levinas have on how we behave, or, rather, how we should behave, towards others and in society? And how and where do we search for new knowledge? We are left with a lot of questions and in this final section I will try to develop some answers to them, to the extent that such answers can be deduced from the above discussion.

There is in society an increasing concern about the consequences of a globalised market economy, such as an increasing gap between rich and poor, irreversible environmental devastations and an increasing pressure towards always more efficiency and cuts in budgets in private as well as public affairs. The critique that is expressed follows a long tradition of critical thought and actions against established power structures and authorities. This critical tradition rests on the works of prominent thinkers, among them Kant, Hegel and Marx: Kant (who, of course, stood on the shoulders of earlier great minds) systematised what we call *critical philosophy*, consisting of continuously applying empirical observations along with logical reasoning to question and restate common ideas of truth. Hegel formulated (also in line with a long philosophical tradition) the structure of *dialectics*, as a pattern in the development of ideas where a *thesis* is countered by its *anti-thesis*, generating a *synthesis*, on a higher level of insight than its two predecessors. Finally, Marx applied both the critical philosophy of Kant and the dialectics of Hegel on the history of economy, appointing the working class as the proper counterforce to the ruling capital owners, who should bring history toward a new, classless society without exploitation of any people. From this tradition, *critical dialectics* has become the normal pattern not only of political contest, but of political discourse in general: opposite views meet in debates and discussions with an aim (although not always expressed explicitly) to arrive at some kind of new and improved insight in the form of a synthesis.

The theory of Marx came to become a decisive support for the political struggle of industrial workers in many countries and, exactly in accordance with his dialectics, there developed a synthesis in the form of a *social democracy* that came to characterise most of Western Europe for a long period. Ironically enough we can thus say that the dissemination of the ideas of Marx has postponed the fulfilment of his own prophecy that capitalism one day will fall.

The ideas of Marx also became a great source of inspiration for other kinds of revolts by suppressed groups – and by their advocates – all over the world. His ideas, however, were also used by those who suppressed others, such as in the former Soviet Union, Eastern Europe, China, and in totalitarian regimes in the Third World. The ideas of Marx were used to develop alternative ideologies to capitalism, ideologies that often were labelled 'Marxism'. Especially at a time with a large faith in science and rationality it was heavily emphasised that Marxism constitutes a 'scientific truth', and great efforts were made to lay a consistent, logical structure onto this ideology, so that it could serve as a theoretical superstructure, whether it was for a revolt of the suppressed or to strengthen the power of the suppressors. In this way Marxism fulfilled the criteria of instrumental knowledge as these are specified in chapter 3: it became, for those who professed it, normative, conventional and logically explicable. But in that way it also became an self-centred knowledge, in the sense described earlier in this book, and that which had been the original ethical initiative in Marx's criticism of capitalism's suppression of the industrial workers disappeared gradually out of sight. This development did not take place everywhere, however, and these differences in applications illustrate exactly what has earlier been said about the consequences of developing instrumental knowledge: in the cases where knowledge became both normative, conventional and explicable, ethics, which may have been the initial cause for developing the knowledge, withered away, as knowledge having these three properties became egocentric. Said otherwise: a sincere wish for a more just world can only partly be supported by rational constructions and systems; there will always have to be an element that this rationality can never conceive: my particular obligation towards the particular other.

In the 1960s and 70s there emerged a new interest in 'the moral Marx', that is, Marx without the totalitarian 'Marxist' ideology. One talked about a neo-Marxism. One outcome of this was the '68 revolt' initiated by French students in May 1968. This revolt became the beginning of a period witnessing various protests against the lack of ethics in the market economy, such as protests against environmental devastation, against the increasing global gap between rich and poor, and also the feminist criticism and revolts against the suppression of women in a capitalist economy. In this way critical dialectics, based on the tradition of Kant, Hegel and Marx as described above, became paradigmatic for various categories of dissents and protests.

What does Levinas bring into this situation? To the method of critical dialectics Levinas would raise the following, disquieting question: in what position am I to criticise the Other by saying that he or she is wrong and that I am right? To Levinas, in the encounter with the Other, the Other is my teacher and my master. In the next turn, though, in society, where there are also other others, I will have to compare and acquire knowledge in order to judge between different postulates and arguments. But still I have no reason to say that the Other is wrong. In fact, wouldn't it be more 'Levinasian' to say that the Other is always right within his or her own (subjective) context? Is not the opinion of another exactly what it must be, considering the social and political context in which it has been generated? And in the same way, what is proposed from *my* critical perspective as an alternative 'truth', isn't that also what it must be, viewed in the context in which my knowledge is generated? What prevents this contextual view on knowledge to end in a total ethical relativism and in the popular view of post-modern language games as an arena where 'anything goes', however, is for Levinas the absolute objectivity of the Other and the call for responsibility from the Other.

As we have seen in earlier chapters, Levinas joins a philosophical tradition where truth cannot be considered independent of language. The method of critical dialectics is not only a way of arriving at higher levels of insight. It is also a linguistic game, constituting the reality it describes, or, to use a philosophical term, constructing an *ontology*. In a response to one of his colleagues who is best known for his rethinking of ontology, Jacques Derrida, Levinas says:

> May not Derrida's work cut into the development of Western thinking with a line of demarcation similar to Kantianism, which separated dogmatic philosophy from critical philosophy? Are we again at the end of a naïveté, of an unsuspected dogmatism which slumbered at the base of that which we took for critical spirit? (Levinas, 1991c: 3)

In order to meet and bring an end to dogmatic thinking, critical dialectics has been, and probably still is, the most successful remedy. Critical dialectics is developed to 'beat' dogmatic thinking. It is a weapon forged for questioning ruling ideas, theories and ideologies, and still saving what is worth saving through a synthesis. Therefore, when this method is applied in the critique of the global market economy it, mostly tacitly, presupposes that business life is also based on some kind of dogmatic ideas, theories and/or ideologies. The apparent lack of effect of these attacks on common business life and the global market economy, however, may be caused by the possible fact that business conduct is *not* based on any dogmatic thought, nor any ideology – it may not even depend on a theory. The consistent theories presented in business textbooks may not be as indispensable to business life as the educators wish to think. Business life is both historically and culturally based on *pragmatics*, not on theory. Economic and business practice does not need any theoretical base; being based on *self-interest* makes it self-sufficient. This property of self-sufficiency is exactly why Levinas chose the economy as the point of departure in his introduction to the Other and to ethics in *Totality and Infinity*: economy is the proper and self-sustained home of the self-interest without need of any reflection, theory or ideology. To Levinas economy is synonymous with ontology, with *the said*, our conception of what there *is*, supported by language. And from this point of departure he proceeded to that which is beyond ontology, or, rather, to that which is 'more ontological than ontology' (Levinas, 1998: 90), that is the Other, who can be experienced only ethically, as responsibility. In other words, if ethics is 'more ontological than ontology', then what has earlier been regarded as 'ontology' must then be something 'less ontological' than what it earlier was considered to be.

What does this mean in terms of consequences? There is, as we know, daily a lot of brutality, violence and killing in the world. But to point at the market economy or capitalism as an explanation for this brutality, or, alternatively, to use it as an excuse, is to consider these constructions as 'more ontological' than their assumed consequences. That would be to take the responsibility away from those who are responsible. Similarly, when the President of the United States uses linguistic constructions such as 'The War against Terrorism' or 'The Gift of Freedom' as reasons to kill many people and to cause great suffering to even more, or when Islamic suicide bombers use 'Jihad' as an explanation for their fatal actions, both obviously consider such construction to be 'more ontological' than what they can possibly be after Levinas. They deny the responsibility that actually *is* 'more ontological' than these linguistic constructions. Although one should have no illusions that neither the President of the United States nor an Islamic suicide bomber will change his or her behaviour as soon as they are confronted with this 'more ontological' responsibility, it may have an effect in more everyday cases if it is acknowledged that the market economy is used as either an explanation or excuse in the moment the responsibility for the consequences are acknowledged as 'more ontological'.

This way of looking at responsibility meets another obstacle in the much used demarcation line that has been drawn between *deontological* (or 'Kantian') and *consequential* (or 'utilitarian') ethics in so many textbook presentations of ethics. This distinction is commonly viewed as two mutually exclusive alternative approaches to ethics. The lesson from Levinas may change this: the presence of the third necessitates great efforts in comparing, calculations and knowledge about consequences and efficiency, very much similar to what we know from applications of utilitarian ethics, as we know from, for instance, cost-benefit analyses. When Levinas emphasises the motivation for just solutions, however, as the call for responsibility from the encounter with the Other, this can hardly be viewed as other than a further elaboration of the deontological ethics within the Kantian tradition. In other words, both elements are necessary, and Levinas has made it possible to leave ontology to economics, language and utilitarianism, while 'real' ethics is a further development of Kant, but placed prior to language. In cases where ethics is perverted it is very often because one has chosen one of these two elements and excluded the other. For instance, an 'ethics of closeness' expresses a responsibility to the Other that excludes the third, while exploitation of workers often following from pursuing efficiency as a virtue avoids the encounter with the individual Other. After Levinas these two 'ethics' do not need to come into conflict with each other because they have different domains of application: calculations, efficiency, consequences and justice belong to the generalised abstractions of society, while responsibility and obligation towards the Other belong to the particular, unique and real events of encounters.

Levinas elaborates on this distinction by denoting the first as *morality* and the latter as *ethics*:

> By morality I mean a series of rules relating to social behaviour and civic duty. But while morality thus operates in the socio-political order of organizing and improving our human survival, it is ultimately founded on an ethical responsibility towards the other. As *prima philosophia*, ethics cannot itself legislate for society or produce rules of conduct whereby society might be revolutionised or transformed. It does not operate at the level of the manifesto or *call to order*; it is not a *savoir vivre*. When I talk of ethics as a 'dis-inter-estedness', I do not mean that it is indifference; I simply mean that it is a form of vigilant passivity to the call of the other, which precedes our interest in being, our *inter-est*, as a being-in-the-world attached to property and appropriating what is other than itself to itself. Morality is what governs the world of political 'inter-estedness', the social interchanges between citizens in a society. Ethics, as the extreme exposure and sensitivity of one subjectivity to another, becomes morality and hardens its skin as soon as we move into the political world of the impersonal 'third' – the world

of government, institutions, tribunals, prisons, schools, committees, and so on. But the norm that must continue to inspire and direct the moral order is the ethical norm of the interhuman. If the moral-political order totally relinquishes its ethical foundation, it must accept all forms of society, including the fascist or totalitarian, for it can no longer evaluate or discriminate between them. The state is usually better than anarchy – but not always. In some instances, – fascism or totalitarianism, for example – the political order of the state may have to be challenged in the name of our ethical responsibility to the other. This is why ethical philosophy must remain the first philosophy. (Levinas, in Levinas and Kearney, 1986: 29-30)

The source of ethics, which is the call of the Other in the singular and physical event of an encounter, can never be carried directly over to some general theory without being reduced. There are in fact lots of ethics in society, wherever people meet, both within and outside organizations, but they disappear too easily as we retreat to ideas and theories. It is the good, prior to any language, and not language itself, that keeps human relations together. Without it, life would be unbearable.

Certainly we, and in particular we who happen to belong to the privileged rich part of the world, find ourselves trapped in power structures in which we are forced to participate, violating others, relations in which we do not want to participate. But that is exactly why the only way to put ethics into practice requires that these consistent structures are revealed as serving the interests of the self and then, after being called by the Other, to make efforts to change these structures, if not more than just a little bit, in the direction of always more justice.

To sum up: Instead of arriving at some ethical prescriptions, for instance in the form of specific answers and guidelines to social and political questions, Levinas starts with recognising and acknowledging economic, self-centred conduct as a universal human need, from which no one can escape, in the sense of positioning oneself above others. Included in this thinking is the need to understand, to comprehend, and to control, by developing instrumental knowledge, as this is described earlier in this book. Then he reminds us that human life is more than economy: there are also the particular events when one is called to responsibility by the Other. And although these events cannot be thematised, their consequences can, which are, as we have described in the previous chapter, efforts towards always more justice.

In an attempt to make this point even more concrete, I will close this book by going back to the example of chapters 3 and 5, with the financial director who is given the task to produce a budget for the hospital within new and more austere financial restrictions set by the top leaders, and the nurse who is responsible for the care in one of the units of the hospital that is obliged to reduce its workforce. Above both these leaders is the general director of the hospital, having a responsibility for the entire institution. His or her instructions to the financial manager should be to produce a just and right budget, in accordance with the mission given to the hospital by society. The budget that is to be elaborated by the financial manager should be regarded as just by those who are involved, and a condition for obtaining this is that everyone has an experience of being met as individuals by their leaders in the concrete encounters during the process. Only then can they accept the brutality of justice, and only then can they contribute by working efficiently, *for* the patient, or, if it had been a private company, *for* the customer. However, this will require from the responsible leaders a sufficiently good professional and substantial knowledge about what the organization is in fact doing. Knowledge in business management alone will not be sufficient. On the other hand, however, no knowledge or theory of any kind will be sufficient. There is no such thing as a system that to a sufficient extent takes care of justice. Systems have to be populated by people who can see the violations caused by the system itself and which in the meeting with others are questioned and thereby struck by the idea of the good and seek to transform this idea into always more justice. This implies constantly moving between mercy and justice, between ethics and ontology. In this lies the necessity of ethics. It requires a human being, no more, no less.

References

Aasland, D. G. (2005) *Økonomiens grenser og etikkens nødvendighet: En vei til Emmanuel Levinas*. Oslo: Cappelen Akademisk Forlag.

Bateson, G. (2002) *Mind and Nature: A Necessary Unity*. Cresskill: Hampton Press.

Bauman, Z. (1989) *Modernity and the Holocaust*. Cambridge: Polity Press.

Buber, M. (1987) *I and Thou*, trans. R. G. Smith. Edinburgh: T. & T. Clark.

Burggraeve, R. (2003) *The Wisdom of Love in the Service of Love: Emmanuel Levinas on Justice, Peace and Human Rights*. Milwaukee: Marquette University Press.

Crane, A. and D. Matten (2004) *Business Ethics*. Oxford: Oxford University Press.

Friedman, M. (1970) 'The social responsibility of business is to increase its profits', *New York Times Magazine*, 13 September 1970: 32-33.

Hancock, J. et al. (1776) 'The unanimous declaration of the thirteen United States of America', *Journals of the Continental Congress*, 5: 510-515.

Ibsen, H. (2001) *The Lady from the Sea*, trans. E. Marx-Aveling. Project Gutenberg, online at www.gutenberg.org/dirs/etext01/ldyse10.txt.

Ibsen, H. (2007) *Peer Gynt*, trans. J. Northam. Ibsen.net, online at ibsen.net/asset/114049/1/114049_1.pdf.

Kuhn, T. (1970) *The Structure of Scientific Revolutions*. Chicago: University of Chicago Press.

Levinas, E. (1985) *Ethics and Infinity: Conversations with Philip Nemo.* Pittsburgh: Duquesne University Press.

Levinas, E. and R. Kearney (1986) 'Dialogue with Emmanuel Levinas', in Cohen, R. (ed.) *Face to Face with Levinas.* New York: SUNY Press.

Levinas, E. (1990) *Difficult Freedom: Essays on Judaism,* trans. S. Hand. London: Athlone.

Levinas, E. (1991a) *Totality and Infinity,* trans. A. Lingis. Dordrecht: Kluwer Academic Publishers.

Levinas, E. (1991b) *Otherwise than Being, or, Beyond Essence,* trans. A. Lingis. Dordrecht: Kluwer Academic Publishers.

Levinas, E. (1991c) 'Wholly otherwise', trans. S. Critchley, in R. Bernasconi and S. Critchley (eds) *Re-Reading Levinas.* Bloomington: Indiana University Press.

Levinas, E. (1998) *Of God who Comes to Mind,* trans. B. Bergo. Stanford: Stanford University Press.

Levinas, E. (2007) 'Sociality and money', trans. F. Bouchetoux and C. Jones, *Business Ethics: A European Review,* 16(3): 203-207.

Løgstrup, K. E. (1997) *The Ethical Demand.* Notre Dame: University of Notre Dame Press.

Lyotard, J.-F. (1984) *The Postmodern Condition : A Report on Knowledge,* trans. G. Bennington and B. Massumi. Manchester: Manchester University Press.

Noddings, N. (1984) *Caring: A Feminine Approach to Ethics and Moral Education.* Berkeley: University of California Press.

Smith, A. (1976) *An Inquiry into the Nature and Causes of the Wealth of Nations,* vol. 2. Oxford: Clarendon Press.

Sonnenfeld, J. A. (2002) 'What makes great boards great?' *Harvard Business Review,* 80(9): 106-113.

Spinoza, B. de (1997) *Ethics,* trans. A. Boyle. London: Dent & Tuttle.

CPSIA information can be obtained
at www.ICGtesting.com
Printed in the USA
LVOW13s2003250218
567844LV00021B/392/P